THE SEASONAL FLORIST

THE SEASONAL FLORIST

Rona Coleman

CHRISTOPHER HELM

A & C Black · London

© 1990 Rona Coleman
Photographs by Alan Turner of Turner Gee Studios,
London
Line illustrations by Shirley Curzon

Christopher Helm (Publishers) Ltd,
Imperial House, 21–25 North Street,
Bromley, Kent BR1 1SD, a subsidiary of
A & C Black (Publishers) Ltd,
35 Bedford Row, London WC1R 4JH

ISBN 0-7136-8013-X

A CIP catalogue record for this book
is available from the British Library

Typeset by Rowland Phototypesetting Ltd,
Bury St Edmunds, Suffolk
Printed and bound in Great Britain
by The Bath Press Ltd, Avon

CONTENTS

AUTUMN

WINTER

COLOUR PLATES

FIGURES

ACKNOWLEDGEMENTS

To my husband, for his inexhaustible tolerance and generous practical help.

To Messrs Baarsen and Company of Aalsmeer, Holland, for so generously providing some of the flowers required for the designs.

To Betty Jones, NDSF, President of the Society of Floristry, for advice on some of the most popular commercial rose varieties.

To Thomas Lim, NDSF, of Singapore, for his enthusiasm for floristry and for creating the bouquets.

To Alan Turner, of Turner Gee Studios, London, for taking the photographs.

INTRODUCTION

The specific date margins of the seasons, as gathered from a reliable diary, surprised me. While the first day of spring is actually 21 March, summer apparently begins with the longest day on 21 June, the onset of autumn is 23 September and winter begins on the shortest day, 22 December.

Although we can divide the year according to the calendar, garden flowers will disregard the date and only prosper and bloom when conditions are right for them. To come into flower each plant species needs a specific level of light, temperature and humidity.

But lovely though our own garden flowers and native wild flowers are, the florist is now able to offer the public a wider choice throughout the year. Flowers now come to us from all over the world, those from the southern hemisphere also allowing us to take advantage of their opposite seasons. Being able to handle these exotic flowers is one of the many exciting aspects of floristry and flower arranging. For special occasions some of the larger exotics are truly magnificent and a few stems make tremendous impact.

Many flowers are produced in the UK, too, out of season by artificially controlling the growing environment. The most perfect conditions possible are produced and maintained inside a glasshouse, regardless of those prevailing outside.

Controlled heating, regular watering, feeding and ventilation all cost money and thus, in relation to garden-grown flowers, those in the shops reflect this capital expenditure. Most flowers are now available all year round but, like out-of-season fruits and vegetables, they cost more when not in their natural season. Daffodils, freesia, tulips, anemones and mimosa are usually on display even before Christmas. At one time, chrysanthemums were the traditional flower for Christmas decoration, both in the home and for church. But, although they still live up to their reputation for lasting for several weeks, in an average home their huge heads can be somewhat overwhelming alongside the Christmas tree and decorations.

Although most flowers can be produced throughout the year there is one interesting exception, the lovely sweet pea. It dislikes being packed and shipped, and is only available in its natural season. True, it continues blooming sometimes well into late July and even August in the gardens, but the long-stemmed specimen flowers are usually only in season in flower shops during May and June.

A flower's journey from producer to consumer is fascinating. It is grown in optimum conditions, quite possibly on another continent. It is cut, graded, packed and shipped to major wholesale markets, from there to be distributed to anywhere in the country. Whilst this takes time, it is not nearly so much as one would imagine. For instance, carnations grown in South America could be on display in British shops three or four days after picking, while roses from Israel take even less time to reach the consumer. Plants from Denmark and Belgium are brought over in huge trucks within 24 hours of an order being placed by the distributor.

PART I

PRACTICAL FLORISTRY

1

THE FLORIST'S SHOP

LAYOUT

The layout of a florist's shop should be flexible enough to take account of variations from season to season. For example, a spring flower display does not need so much space as summer and autumn flowers. The ideal situation is for some of your shelves and display stands to be mobile, so that they can be expanded or packed away as the season dictates.

Mirrors are ideal for creating an impression of space. However, some of the plant display units used so lavishly and expensively by some store fitters have, in my view, just the reverse effect. They seem to emphasise the limitations of the display whereas, were the plants carefully grouped at varying heights, the effect would be less regimented.

It is essential to have a good floor that is comfortable to work on, for a busy florist covers quite a few miles moving around the shop in one day. It must tolerate water spillage and, of course, stand up to constant wear. Heavy duty carpet tiles are good because any areas of wear can be replaced. Cork tiling is also very long-lasting. Do not economise on flooring; none of it is cheap and labour costs are the same to lay a more durable one. It would be infuriating to have it relaid within a matter of a few years.

Aim for an even heat throughout, for your own comfort and to keep flowers in prime condition. A good working temperature is between 10 and 15°C. Your local heating council will advise you—but do not install gas as this will have a bad effect on the flowers.

It may be necessary to seek advice from experts about light as well, but beware of being sold a lighting system which proves unsuitable for your particular business. Spotlights need to be individually controlled and adjustable.

Before finalising the placement of display fixtures, the cash register, the card and writing table and the wrapping area try walking into the shop as if you are a customer. Once inside, in which direction do you walk? Is there any feature that seems to dictate customer flow? It is absolutely essential to see the shop from the customers' point of view; and also try to visit other shops to see what seems to work and what does not appeal to you.

A shop in Germany has simulated a woodland glade in the first 3 m or so inside the entrance. Against the walls, on either side, are very large foliage plants, even some young trees as well. These are graded down to smaller ones towards the front. The displays are not solid, being interspersed with small areas of moss and stones. Customer flow was indicated by a wide pathway edged with a colourful border of smaller pot plants such as polyanthus, cineraria and saintpaulia. In a busy city, this rustic display was wonderfully appealing and, at the same time, ensured that the customers walked right to the back of the shop where the cut flowers were displayed.

At peak times, for example for Mothering Sunday and at Christmas, the florist will need to increase display space, but it must not be at the expense of customer space, for more of this will be needed as well. Boxes of plants placed on the shop floor are not only hazardous for the public but dangerous for the plants as well.

So how can this need for temporary extra space be overcome? Cut flowers will obviously come in day by day as required and it is usually possible to arrange to receive the plants in two or three batches. The alternative is to rent other accommodation, if there happens to be some fairly near the shop—a village hall, for instance, or an empty shop.

BUYING

For the newly established florist, buying is probably the greatest enigma of all. Whether buying for your own shop or as the representative of a large concern, it is a challenge as well as a heavy responsibility. It is also a technique that can only really be learnt by experience.

The market for which you are aiming will dictate what to buy to a certain extent. For the lower end of the market look for cheaper flowers, probably pre-packed, but for an up-market appeal look for quality in everything. The flowers will cost more but the public is now very discerning and is conditioned to expect quality in everything they buy.

On your first buying list should be regular lines such as carnations, seasonal flowers and cut foliage and some unusual items which will add distinction to your display. Do not be disappointed if you do not sell the more unusual items. They are vital to your display, for they will encourage people to look at your window and this is the preliminary stage to buying.

Another point to bear in mind is that some flowers develop from bud to full bloom more quickly than others. Daffodils expand particularly quickly, but resist the temptation to buy in very tight bud, in what is known as the 'pencil' stage, since they may not open. They should usually be bought in the 'goose neck' stage unless they are needed to show full colour immediately.

Tulips and iris should be in bud, but showing a little colour. The iris in Plate 2 had been in water for 24 hours. Freesia travels better in bud but the lowest bloom should be showing colour and the same applies to gladioli.

Carnations are available both in tight bud and full bloom. It is a matter of preference how you buy them, but bear in mind that when in bud they can take several days to expand to the full bloom. The buyer has to decide when the flower will be suitable for whatever work is on hand. Gift bouquets, for example, must contain flowers with maximum potential vase life while funeral work requires more instant colour impact and, therefore, more mature flowers.

Roses should always be bought in bud for most varieties expand to full flower fairly quickly. Even so, the bud itself ought to be showing colour and not appear too pinched.

Keep a diary of what you buy, when and where, and how much you pay. This may seem a lot of work at the outset but for next year, and particularly at peak seasons, you will find this record invaluable in assessing your future requirements.

Date _____ Paid cash or cheque

REQUIREMENTS			BOUGHT			
Essentials	Substitute	Extras	From	Quantity	Variety	Price

Flower	Stem count	Comments
Alstroemeria	5 or 10	
Anemone	5 or 10	
Carnation	20 or 25	usually all one colour
Spray	5 or 10	
Chrysanthemum large blooms		boxes of from 15–30 flowers, according to size of bloom
spray	5, 10 or 15	
Daffodil	10	boxes of 30–40 bunches
Freesia	5 or 10	five bunches to one bundle
Gerbera		boxes of usually 30 blooms, rarely mixed, sometimes two colours, but usually all one
Gladioli	5 or 10	one colour only
Iris	5 or 10	in bundles of 50 stems [all one colour]
Liatris	5 or 10	in bundles of 50 stems
Rose	10 or 20	one colour only
Tulip	5 or 10	minimum purchase is usually five bunches, while boxes contain about 30 bunches

The suggested buying sheet on page 6 indicates the most important points. Fix the sheets to a clipboard and attach a ballpoint pen.

Above all, keep a flexible attitude of mind about your purchases. It could be that an item you regard as essential has not arrived, or is poor quality. You must be ready to switch ideas no matter how early it is in the morning.

Most professional florists buy their materials from a wholesale market, or from visiting wholesalers, or from both sources. Buying from the wholesale market means exactly that: there are certain arbitrary counts, or amounts (see below), so it must rest with your supplier whether he will diminish these counts or not. If he does, you must expect to pay more than if you bought the total.

If you are ordering by telephone, be perfectly clear as to whether you are ordering numbers of stems or numbers of bunches.

The difference could be alarming. The above table is an approximate guide, bearing in mind that counts can vary slightly from one grower to another and also according to the country of origin.

WASTAGE

There will be times when flowers must be thrown away and one has to learn to recognise when a flower no longer has any value in the shop. Some flowers mature more quickly than others and some, such as carnations and chrysanthemums, remain in a state of maturity far longer than, say, daffodils and scabious which can literally collapse in a matter of hours. Throwing flowers away does not necessarily mean that they have not earned money.

Take as an example, the purchase of a bundle of 50 stems of iris. Half are sold as cut flowers on the first day. During the next two days no 'cut flowers' are sold but 15 are included in sympathy tributes. So, from the original bundle of 50 stems, only 10 are left unused. These will be at total maturity after three days yet may still be included in a display arrangement for the shop. After a further two or three days, the arrangement will no longer do you credit so it is thrown away.

This is not wastage, for the flowers have been working for you in the arrangement. Had the 15 flowers used in sympathy tributes been thrown away instead, then this would certainly count as wastage—completely different from waste. The first is unavoidable, due to materials not being used while the second implies carelessness. The first is a reasonable business hazard but the second should be avoided at all costs.

Some florists like to keep a check of everything that has to be thrown away; this may work in some organisations, particularly where there are numerous operators. But in the smaller environment keeping a waste list is both time-consuming and, in the main, counter-productive.

One really hard lesson to learn about buying and wastage is not to be downcast when one has made a mistake by over-buying, or of buying the wrong thing. Mark it down to experience and maintain a good relationship with your bank manager!

EXAMINATIONS

Is it necessary to pass examinations in order to be a successful florist? There are differing opinions on this burning question. On the one hand, there are florists who are operating very successfully, and have been doing so for a number of years, without any paper qualifications. Their ability has been founded on years of experience in every facet of the industry. More than likely they are principals in their own establishments, so that annual turnover is the barometer of success or failure. They have built up goodwill over long years which, possibly, might have been theirs more quickly if original enthusiasm and dedication could have been allied to formal training and subsequent examination standards; though this is pure supposition, for until about thirty years ago there was almost no formal training available.

However, now that training is available nationwide, all staff wanting to work anywhere in Britain or, indeed, overseas, should aim to possess that piece of paper that indicates they have measured their abilities against a recognised national standard. One other valid reason for taking examinations is that, should you intend to teach, it is vital that you are able to offer your students the highest possible national qualifications plus evidence of a teaching diploma. Good teachers, in my opinion, are made, not born.

2

FLORISTRY EQUIPMENT

In floristry and flower arranging, as in so many other activities, it helps tremendously to have the right tools and accessories. As far as personal equipment is concerned, you should buy the very best you can afford.

Florists' Shears
These must be chosen according to personal preference and should not be heavy or badly balanced. There are several on the market that are well-balanced, light in weight and have long blades and large finger holes. All these points are essential for comfortable working. Wilkinson produce shears that conform in all these aspects but there are others that are similar in design and which are quite modest in price. If you are left-handed, there are shears made especially for you.

A good pair of shears will cut most average-sized stems, as well as wires and ribbons. However, some foliage is too heavy for either scissors or shears, and so a second pair of heavy-duty cutters is helpful. The ones I rely on are by Wilkinson and can do everything except cut ribbon neatly.

Whether buying for yourself or for shop staff, do steer clear of the small, so-called 'snips'. They are strangely heavy in relation to their size, have small finger holes and soon become blunt and out of alignment. Inferior scissors hurt your hands and slow down work.

Knives
It is important that knives are also well-balanced and easy to use. One of the most comfortable is the short-bladed one with an orange handle that is sold by most wholesalers. This knife is cheap and can be sharpened when necessary. It has a fixed blade which makes it dangerous to keep in a pocket unguarded. For greater safety try digging the tip into a bottle cork.

It is vital to keep tools clean. Shine the blades of both shears and knife with steel wool from time to time, and they will be easier to use and less likely to convey bacteria from stem to stem.

Containers
Most enthusiastic flower arrangers have a fascinating range of containers. They add to their collection by visits to antique fairs, auctions and the bric-à-brac stall at local fêtes. If possible, the container should be attractive, even without flowers. The old-fashioned boat-shaped vases of the 1950s were almost impossible to use, being very wide at the neck and greedy for flowers. Worse still, they were very ugly when not camouflaged with flowers and foliage. In contrast, the handmade pottery pitcher in Plate 6 is an example which arrests the eye even when empty. The depth of water and narrow neck make it ideal for tall garden flowers—foxgloves as illustrated their long stems deep into the water or, perhaps, early delphiniums. All this for just a few moments spent in cutting and placing, for 'arranging' is too extravagant a word. Long-stemmed tulips or mimosa would also look comfortable in this container.

For the florist, the range of stock carried will be limited by how much it is possible to invest. A certain number of containers are essential for display and also smaller ones for gift arrangements. As few of these arrangements as possible should be set in plastic saucers since these are really only intended to be inner containers. A balance has to be struck between stocking minimum quantities and having large amounts of stock which tie up shelf space and cash.

Floral Foam

Floral foam comes in bricks, squares and rounds. It can be fixed to the container using prongs (or frogs as they are sometimes called) or Oasis-fix which is an oil-based adhesive. This should be used sparingly and kept cool.

The boxes of each shape of foam can take up quite a lot of space in the florist's shop but one cannot afford to be short of this basic product.

Flower Preservative

This is available to both amateur and professional alike. For the florist it can be purchased in small sachets to accompany gift bouquets or in small drums for use in the workroom. It should be used not only for conditioning flowers but also to soak the foam used in arrangements.

Wire

A good selection of wire is essential for the florist. It is by no means cheap, so care must be taken to keep every gauge in separate containers, suitably labelled. Most bundles of wire are labelled with the metric measurement, some indicate both metric and standard wire gauge figures, some still only carry the latter figure, so it is useful to know the equivalent measurements.

The strongest is the 1.25 mm size while the finest is 0.20 mm. Those from 0.46 to 0.20 mm are available in silver as well as the

regular blue annealed. Silver wires are used for wiring foliage and for any white, cream or pale colour flowers that might show a mark. A green finish which is more pleasant to use and does not rust is available for wires from 0.46 to 1.25 mm. Quantities of each gauge needed will depend on the type of work done, although it is unlikely that many of the 1.25 and 1 mm gauges will be needed now that many florists use foam funeral bases. Reel or bobbin wire is useful for binding moss to wire frames and for securing bouquets. In general, use 0.56 or 0.46 mm annealed wire for the heavier work and 0.28 or 0.24 mm silver wire for bouquets and ribbons. The very finest wire, 0.20 mm, is needed for wiring lily-of-the-valley, so keep at least one bundle of this gauge in stock.

Florist's Tape

This is a finishing tape used for sealing the end of the stem or the base of a flower after it has been wired for inclusion in boutonnieres, lapel sprays and bouquets. It is available in a number of colours, including several shades of green, brown, black, scarlet and pastel tints. The green is most popular as it still maintains the natural appearance of a design. Splitting the tape in half gives a neater, more delicate look to the work. Whether or not you use gutta-percha is a matter of preference. It does not need to be split as it stretches quite a lot when applied under tension. All tape should be stored in a cool place, otherwise it may become sticky.

Raffia

Raffia, or plastic string, is used for binding presentation bouquets. However, for very delicate or brittle stems, use wool which will stretch and grip the stems without cutting into them.

Ribbons

This is an exciting area of equipment for, as

Mm	Standard wire gauge	Mm	Standard wire gauge
1.25	18	0.38	28
1.00	19	0.32	30
0.90	20	0.28	32
0.70	22	0.24	34
0.56	24	0.20	36
0.46	26		

well as the basic colours and textures, there are now a multitude of unusual designs. There are so many, in fact, that it makes a specific selection very difficult. The basic range must be a suitable selection of polypropylene ones of the best quality which, at a distance, look like regular satin ribbon. A lot of the harsher ribbons are still obtainable. They are of a heavy paper-like texture and the softer ones are well worth the slightly extra cost. These are fine for trimmings and gift wrap in general, but water-resistant satin ribbon should be used for any extra-special presentation and for all bridal work.

Wrapping Paper and Clear Plastic

It is not really essential to have paper overprinted as this usually involves ordering a substantial number of rolls resulting in considerable capital expenditure.

Dusters

A number of clean dusters are vital in the flower shop. Droplets of water on work surfaces are unavoidable but they should be dried as soon as possible to avoid their marking a clean piece of wrapping paper or a design book.

Sprayers

These are obtainable in various sizes, shapes and prices. It is essential to have one which is reliable and produces a fine mist. A hose-type sprayer attached to the workroom tap is generally very efficient, but can sometimes result in a 'traffic jam' at very busy periods.

Plastic Store Containers

Intended only for conditioning flowers and definitely not for display, these are usually dark green and come in at least two sizes.

Glue Gun

This is a DIY tool that is now widely used by florists and flower arrangers. There are numerous designs and some are quite reasonably priced while others are very expensive. Some of the cheaper models drip, which is wasteful of the glue sticks and very untidy. One of the neatest is made by Black & Decker.

Only a minute dab of glue is needed and rapid work is essential because the glue dries almost at once. It is also extremely hot, so beware of finger burns.

The glue gun is ideal for working with dried and everlasting materials, attaching dry foam to other foam or bases, securing ribbon bows and, should a flower get accidentally dislodged from a finished design, another can be neatly fixed on without having to undo the design. A glue gun should never take the place of traditional methods of floristry, such as wiring, taping and binding, but should be regarded as a very useful accessory.

Stationery

Order pads must be of good quality and be printed with the name of your firm, the address and telephone number. This means a large initial outlay but, strangely, the public is more aware of an attractive document than of wrapping paper, which is so soon thrown away. Make sure that the pen you use has a fine enough point to write a carbon copy clearly for, when writing an order in duplicate or taking a relay order, the second copy needs to be as clear as the first.

Message cards and envelopes for every occasion must be available at the appropriate time. If cards are ordered in sufficient quantity, some suppliers will print your name and address on the reverse side. Ideally you should have several designs for birthdays and anniversaries, good luck greetings, several with more general greetings, plus those for special occasions such as St Valentine's Day, Easter, Christmas and Mothering Sunday.

3

CONDITIONING THE FLOWERS

It is essential that flowers and foliage should be properly cared for so that they last as long as possible. This is known as conditioning which Anthony Gatrell, in his dictionary of floristry and flower arranging, defines as 'the careful treatment of fresh cut, living plant material in order to preserve freshness and so prolong its life by various means so that stems take up water more easily'. Emphasis should be placed on the word 'careful' for it is not always simply a matter of cutting off a piece of stem and standing the material in water.

FLOWERS FROM THE FLORIST

Flowers received as a gift bouquet, or bought from the florist, should already have been conditioned. Yet the stem ends will have calloused over very quickly—this is the flower's defence mechanism against completely drying out. Therefore, before arranging them at home, the stem ends should again be cut with a sharp knife and the flowers placed in a lukewarm nutrient solution for at least 30 minutes.

The florist will probably have included a sachet of flower food with the flowers and the instructions on the packet should be followed.

FLOWERS FROM THE GARDEN

If convenient, take a container with a little water, or some nutrient solution, around the garden with you when cutting flowers and foliage. Alternatively, prepare the container beforehand so that they can be put in to condition at the earliest possible moment. Leave them for several hours before arranging. Some foliage such as hostas, will benefit from being completely submerged.

IN THE FLORIST'S SHOP

Prepare the containers, first making sure that they are completely clean. Mix a solution of flower food (Chrysal) in lukewarm water, following the instructions on the packet or drum. If the weather is very warm use cold water but, in general, this proves too much of a shock to the flower stems.

Make sure that you have chosen an appropriate container for the flowers. A deep, straight-sided one is needed for very long-stemmed subjects such as alstroemeria and gladiolus. Freesias and anemones need a shorter, narrower vase. Even when conditioning flowers for storage rather than display, it is vital to use the right container so that blooms do not become crushed or submerged in the water. No more than about 10 cm of water is needed because the stems usually only take up water from the tip.

The majority of flowers will react favourably to a basic conditioning technique. The stems should be cut at an angle with a sharp knife and never with scissors for, however sharp and clean they are, they can constrict the vascular tubes and thus prevent the stem from taking up water. The blooms should then stand in the lukewarm flower food solution for a few hours. Some species need special treatment or longer conditioning.

ANEMONE Cut the stem ends and stand the bunches facing inwards so that the stems straighten as they take up water. Keep them in the dark or, at least, well away from strong light otherwise the flowers will expand very quickly. Anemones remain in full flower for several days. If removed at night to a cool, dark place the open flowers will close up.

ANTHURIUM Remove each stem carefully from its water phial. Cut stem end and stand the flowers in lukewarm nutrient solution. Make sure the flower heads do not swing around and become damaged. If necessary, place a small roll of paper between each one so that the heads do not touch each other.

BOUVARDIA The flower buds should be about 75 per cent developed. Defoliate lower stem, cut as usual and stand in warm flower food solution. In winter, use only half the prescribed dosage of flower food. Store at about 15°C.

CARNATION Remove lower foliage and cut stem just above a node. Stand in lukewarm nutrient solution and leave in the open. Never store carnations in a closed situation. Check every day for petal-curl in the mature blooms.

CHRYSANTHEMUM Remove lower leaves; cut stem end with sharp knife and stand in warm Chrysal solution. Never hammer stems, for they will pollute the water.

DAFFODIL AND NARCISSUS Stand in cold water solution of Daffodil-Chrysal. Store away from strong light, unless you want the flowers to open quickly.

EREMURUS Condition for at least 48 hours, otherwise the flower tip will not remain upright.

EUPHORBIA FULGENS Do not cut stem ends, but stand them in 5 cm of hot water for a few moments. Bring out and cut, as usual, in the centre of the length of stem which has been submerged. Stand in warm Chrysal solution and store in an even temperature of about 15°C.

FOLIAGE Cut stem ends and condition in a warm solution of shrub nutrient.

FREESIA Remove clear plastic sleeves; also remove covering of cotton wool on stem ends. Stand in 7 cm of lukewarm Chrysal solution.

GERBERA They require only a maximum of 8 cm of Chrysal solution. Do not allow stems to droop over the side of the container, for if they take up water when curved, they will never straighten up. If necessary, wrap them very loosely in clean paper so that they remain upright. Leave to condition away from strong light, for two to three days. They should be stored at an even temperature of about 15°C. They will not tolerate cold conditions.

GLADIOLUS Remove lower foliage and cut at least 3 cm off the stem. Stand in a tall container and place in a light situation so that the flowers can expand.

GYPSOPHILA This is usually very tightly packed, so de-bunch it, clean the stems and cut as usual. Gently shake the flower heads free as they tend to tangle when packed for market. If the flowers are well-developed give them a top spray of Clear-Life, which will help prolong them. But if the bunch is buddy, do not spray, as then the buds will not develop to full flower.

IRIS Remove rubber bands by cutting; do not slide them off the bunch as this may damage both foliage and stems. Do not squash too many into one container as the flowers will need head space to expand.

LIATRIS Remove foliage as for lily. Cut stem end and stand in lukewarm nutrient solution. No need to store in the dark but the position should be draught-free.

LILAC AND SNOWBALL (*Viburnum opulus*) Cut stem ends and remove all foliage. Stand in near-hot shrub food solution. Leave flower heads wrapped until steam from the water stops rising. Store away from any draught.

LILY Strip away foliage from stem to depth of about 13 cm. Cut stem end and stand in lukewarm nutrient solution, making sure that there is enough head space for the flowers to develop comfortably.

LILY-OF-THE-VALLEY The imported and out-of-season flowers arrive in bunches of 10 stems still on the root ball. Cut off, leaving as much stem as convenient. For bridal work, wire each stem, then stand in Chrysal solution and condition for 24 hours. Outdoor-grown lily-of-the-valley should be conditioned in lukewarm nutrient solution, choosing a fairly deep container so that the flowers are totally protected from all draughts.

MOLUCELLA This usually arrives already defoliated. Cut stem ends and stand in lukewarm Chrysal solution. Store well away from draught and in a temperature of not less than 15°C, otherwise the lovely flower heads may keel over.

NERINE Allow several days for flowers to expand to their full colour and beauty. Meanwhile keep in a light situation out of draughts.

ROSE Defoliate lower stems and, if flowers are intended for arrangements and sale, carefully de-thorn the stems. Try not to cut the stem while de-thorning, as this will leave a scar through which bacteria can enter.

If the roses are intended for bridal work and so are cut down to a shorter stem length de-thorning is not necessary. Stand them in warm nutrient solution. Top spray with clean cold water, particularly over the foliage. Store in the cooler or away from draughts and strong light.

SINGAPORE ORCHID These usually arrive in the market in bunches of ten stems, each one in its own small water tube. Remove these tubes and cut the stem ends. Then stand them in lukewarm nutrient solution, making sure that none of the flowers is below water level. Store in an even temperature of not less than 10°C.

STEPHANOTIS Wire and tape. Place in a plastic bag or box, lightly spray and store away from light until needed. Do not put the flowers in water at all before wiring but they can be immersed head-down for a short while after they have been taped and before being stored.

TULIP Remove any plastic wrapping. Cut stem ends and remove any damaged foliage. Stand in 10 cm of very lukewarm tulip solution taking care that no flowers droop over the side of the container. If the stems tend to curve, stand the bunches facing one another inwards and store for a few hours in the dark. They will soon become upright as the stems take up water.

4

WIRING METHODS

Wiring has changed remarkably over recent years for the effect required is now far more natural. Furthermore, many flowers are more durable and there is no need to wire a flower that is perfectly capable of standing up by itself. The object of wiring now is to support the stem and bloom very discreetly, so that the flower is not at risk from handling or the weather, and yet the design still looks as natural as possible. Flowers which are over-wired present a really old-fashioned and down-market appearance.

Deciding which wires to use depends on several factors—such as where the flower will be in the design, or if it will be subjected to windy weather, when a slightly heavier wire would help. Try always to use the lightest wire you think is feasible. If it proves insufficient, you can always extract it and insert a heavier one, never the other way around as by then the fabric of the flower will have been damaged. It is also possible that the wire suited to the flower will not be supportive enough for your design. In that case, give the flower the wire it needs and add another one to the stem so that you then have control over it. (See Table of Gauges, p. 10.)

Sometimes a firm finish is essential, at other times something far lighter is acceptable: both are correct in their individual situations. For example, it would be useless to make a very lightly wired posy for a young bridesmaid when the weather is windy. Alternatively, a lapel spray to be worn on a light material should have minimum support to keep it in control. Both designs might contain the same flowers, but they would be wired differently.

As a general guide to wiring decisions, flowers can be divided approximately into three groups, according to their physical attributes:

(1) Flowers with a strong calyx, such as rose and carnation.
(2) Those with a small calyx relative to the size of the bloom, e.g. chrysanthemum, dahlia.
(3) Flowers with little or no calyx, such as tulip, hyacinth, orchid.

The character of stems also falls into approximately three groups:

(1) Hardy or woody stems, such as rose and chrysanthemum.
(2) Hollow stems as in daffodil, zinnia, cornflower and ranunculus.
(3) Semi-hollow stems, such as tulip and iris.

WIRING FOLIAGE
Stitch Method

Many different ivies are used extensively by florists, mainly because the leaves are so reliable. The method used can be followed for other, similar types of foliage.

First cut leaf stem to a length of about 2 cm. With the underside of the leaf towards you, insert 0.32 mm silver wire at an angle finely across the central vein, about two-thirds of the way up the leaf (see figure 1).

Grasp the leaf firmly between finger and thumb at the point where the wire is inserted. This prevents the wire from moving and making the two tiny holes any larger. Make sure these two holes are not in line for, if they are, they might possibly tear across.

Draw the two ends of wire down parallel

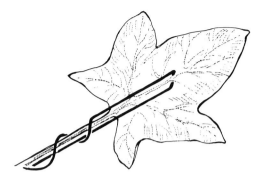

1. *Wiring an ivy leaf by the stitch method*

with each other, one either side of the central vein. Move your grip to the end of the leaf, just at the point where it joins the stem. Then wind one end of wire around the other and also around the leaf stem, twice only. Once wired, taped and stored in a plastic bag or box, ivy foliage will last for at least five days.

Rose Foliage

Choose two leaves as near to the same size as possible. Lay them one on the other, not back to back but both facing the same way. Stitch them through as described for ivy foliage. Since most commercial rose foliage is rather thin, putting two leaves together will give them more 'body' and they will consequently last far longer. Rose foliage will last about two days after wiring. Garden roses usually have wonderfully strong foliage, so it may not always be necessary to put two leaves together.

Sellotape Method

The stitch method is valid for most foliage but waxy and heavy-textured leaves, such as stephanotis, tradescantia, zebrina and chlorophytum, should not be pierced with wire. They can be supported with Sellotape instead.

First make sure that the foliage, your hands and the workbench are all completely dry. Double the 0.32 mm silver wire and lay

it in line with the central vein. Fix with a strip of Sellotape. For chlorophytum, which is an exceptionally long leaf, it will be necessary to add a second wire to continue the support. For broader leaves such as scindapsus and philodendron, add a second strip of Sellotape across the leaf at an angle for added support. The Sellotape should not peel off even when the design is sprayed.

EXTERNAL WIRING

A carnation is the best flower on which to begin wiring practice, since it has a good solid calyx and the bloom is not easily shattered.

Take the wire in one hand, the flower in the other, holding it just under the flower head with the stem hanging downwards. Hold the wire parallel to the flower stem with the point aimed at the underneath of the calyx (see figure 2). Keeping the wire close to and still parallel to the stem insert the tip into the calyx. Drive it up until you

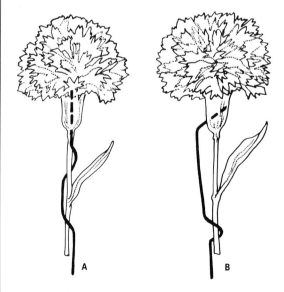

2. *External wiring—insert the wire at the base of the calyx and parallel to it and not at right angles*

feel a slight check as it comes into contact with the seed pod within the bloom. The long end of wire can then be gently stroked round and down the stem at an angle of 45°. Do not twist too much otherwise the stem will be too constricted and will resemble a corkscrew.

Assuming that the flower stem is strong and firm, a 0.56 or 0.70 mm wire should be sufficient. If, on the other hand, the stem is whippy and the flower is to be used more or less at full stem length, it will be necessary to use a 0.90 mm gauge. Never hold the wire at right angles to the stem, for if you insert it and then 'change gear' to wind the wire around the stem, you may disturb the petal formation. At worst, the flower may shatter; at best, it will not last so long. All wires should be inserted sharply and cleanly and not moved around in the flower.

INTERNAL WIRING

From the design point of view, this is the most satisfactory way of wiring flowers, for the wire is inserted inside the stem and is therefore completely invisible.

Hook Method

The wire can be driven upwards through the stem from the end, right into the flower and beyond (see figure 3). Make a small hook and then gently retract the wire so that the hook rests within the flower. Take great care not to pull the hook down too far, otherwise it may puncture the flower petals. This is most important when wiring stephanotis and hyacinth.

The wire can be inserted from the top downwards, but one has to be very careful that the flower stem is perfectly straight and that the wire does not come through the side of it. Daffodils and gerbera, particularly, may be wired with this method. The hook will disappear right down into the daffodil trumpet, but make certain with the gerbera that the wire has completely

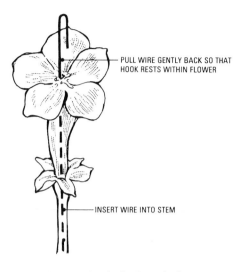

PULL WIRE GENTLY BACK SO THAT HOOK RESTS WITHIN FLOWER

INSERT WIRE INTO STEM

3. *Internal wiring by the hook method*

vanished. A gentle push with the flat blade of your knife will usually take care of it.

Other Methods

Not all flowers with hollow stems can be wired with the hook method; for example, anemone-centred spray chrysanthemum. Even though you use a green wire, the hook will be visible right across the centre of the flower. To wire on a stem-length of about 10–15 cm, say, for a bridal posy or presentation bouquet, insert a wire right up to the flower head. Place your finger on the centre of the flower and if the wire pricks it, you know you have gone a fraction too far. Yet you must ensure that the wire does, in fact, penetrate the flower head and not beyond, for once the flower is bound into the design it is impossible to push the wire back out of sight or to cut it off. Similarly, should the wire not be inserted high enough, the flower will not be supported and may droop, thus spoiling the appearance of the design.

The first wire will support the flower but spray chrysanthemum usually have very hollow stems and so the wire has no real anchorage and may drop out. Therefore, insert a second wire into the stem as far as possible, maybe for only about 2 cm, to block the stem and prevent the first wire from moving.

Flowers to be used for a sympathy tribute, for example, will need to be wired on a much shorter stem. Hold the flower upside-down between finger and thumb and drive the wire through the calyx (see figure 4). While still holding the flower very firmly, pull the two wires down parallel with the stem. Then twist one end of wire twice around the other and the flower stem, as for the ivy foliage. This is not an ideal method as the wire pierces the flower twice which is bound to hasten dehydration, but it sometimes must be used.

A third technique of wiring is to combine the previous two methods. This has to be done when the stem is not smooth but, rather, is punctuated with nodes or joints where a leaf is attached to the stem. It is not possible to get a wire through this spot, so it must be inserted above the node and then twisted around the stem below it as far as is

needed. Iris and tulip stems should be wired like this. One can, of course, insert the wire externally directly into the flower, as for a carnation, but if it is possible to insert it lower down, then this will be far more discreet.

TECHNIQUES FOR INDIVIDUAL FLOWERS

Rose Pinning

This is a method of keeping a bud rose from opening in very warm bright weather.

Cut some silver 0.32 or 0.38 mm wire into short lengths, about 2 cm long. Bend them into tiny hairpins. Before the roses are conditioned and when the flower is comparatively limp, very carefully fold each sepal towards the bud, holding the flower upside-down, and insert the hairpin vertically into the fattest part of the bud (see figure 5). Too low and the hair pin will be useless; too high and it will not look nice at all. Insert a hairpin into all five of the sepals, taking great care not to crack the sepal as you fold it towards the petals. This expedient is only valid for roses that are going to be used in bouquets or other similar designs. It is not suitable for roses that are sold on the stem. Neither is it essential to pin every rose for a design for this will look unnatural. It is attractive if several are left to open as they will, but it is convenient, for

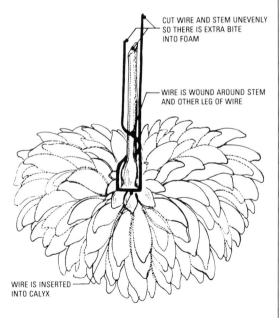

CUT WIRE AND STEM UNEVENLY SO THERE IS EXTRA BITE INTO FOAM

WIRE IS WOUND AROUND STEM AND OTHER LEG OF WIRE

WIRE IS INSERTED INTO CALYX

4. *Wiring a flower on a short stem*

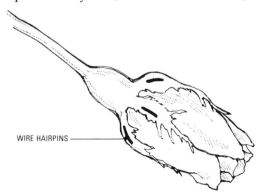

WIRE HAIRPINS

5. *Rose pinning to keep a bud from opening*

instance, to pin those that are describing a line.

Stephanotis

Stephanotis should be wired internally before being conditioned, by inserting a 0.46 mm silver wire up through the stem into the flower using the hook method. Cut each stem to about 2 cm and the wire should go in quite easily. Hold the flower firmly otherwise you may accidentally pop it out of its tiny calyx. Tape it just where the wire joins the tiny stem and then immerse in a bowl of clean water. When all the flowers are wired and taped, store them in a plastic bag or box, seal and put in a dark cool place. They should last at least three days.

Lily-of-the-valley

This is wired before conditioning from the base of the flower stem upwards to the top floret. On arrival, cut the stems off the root ball and wire with 0.20 or 0.24 mm silver wire (see figure 6), leaving about 6 cm of wire loose at the base of the flower head. Then condition in a little lukewarm nutrient solution. To mount each stem ready for a bouquet, cut the stem to the required length. Insert a 0.56 mm silver wire into the stem as far up as possible. Hold a leaf against the stem and bind it on with the spare silver wire left at the base of the flower head. Wind the wire down the stem and on to the mount wire, thus securing it. Tape firmly with full width tape. Lay each prepared flower on a damp towel. Do not stand them in a block of foam or a container for the flowers will then be at risk from draught and any water in the flower head is liable to drain away. Lily-of-the-valley is too beautiful and expensive to risk losing even one flower.

Freesia

The individual florets can be wired with the hook method, but the flower fabric is not so durable as stephanotis or hyacinth and

WIND WIRE AROUND JUST BELOW TOP BUD

LEAVE A LITTLE SPARE WIRE

6. *Initial wiring for lily-of-the-valley*

tends to dehydrate rather quickly. Even so, they are very popular both for lapel sprays and head-dresses, and there are three possible ways of wiring them.

First of all, tape the top 1 cm of a silver wire, 0.38 or 0.46 mm, with pale green half-tape. Make a hook, insert the wire down through the flower with the taped hook just resting inside it.

Alternatively, make the hook and attach a tiny piece of cotton wool to it. Dip it into clean water and insert into the flower. The taped wire, or the cotton wool, will help protect the flower fabric as you overtape it. Also the damp cotton wool will prevent dehydration. The previous method is far quicker though, since the taped 'stamens' can be prepared in advance and kept in a clean jar with a lid, all ready to be used.

Another technique would be to tape the base of the flower, having first removed the calyx. Make a loop with 0.38 mm silver wire, lay it against the floret and bind the longer end of wire twice around the floret and itself. This is a useful technique when the material will not tolerate being pierced but it is not ideal since it gives little support to the flower. The loop method, as it is known, is used for securing tiny groups of petals, when making a carnation 'floret', for example, or for a rolled rose or cyclamen petal.

Orchids

Try to wire all orchids internally. *Cattleya*, *Cymbidium* and *Cyprepedium* orchids have heavy fleshy stems and usually need surprisingly heavy wire, for example 0.70 or 0.90 mm. Sometimes the flower is delicate and yet the stem is still heavy, so the flower must first be wired with a 0.56 mm wire using the hook method and then a second wire, probably 0.70 or 0.90 mm, is inserted to control the stem. A fresh orchid should be springy and the lip will bounce back into position once the hook has been safely recessed into the flower. *Vanda*, *Phalaenopsis* and *Odontoglossum* orchids are much more delicate and should be wired with extreme care. One method is to tape a silver 0.38 mm wire with half-tape, double it and gently place it across the centre of the orchid, bringing the two legs of wire parallel to the stem. Alternatively, insert a silver 0.32 mm into the stem just under the back petal. Twist it around the stem taking extreme care not to damage the fragile petals. Most types of Singapore orchids can be wired by this external method, for the stem is usually too curved just behind the flower to accept the internal method.

Roses

Those on very short stems, to be used for a shoulder or lapel spray, or a head-dress, will usually accept the internal hook method. This is not appropriate for white or pale tinted flowers, since the wire might show. For these, use the double-wire method by inserting one wire right up into the flower head and adding a second one which blocks the stem, so that both are firm within the flower.

Roses to be used on longer stems, for bouquets, posies and presentation designs, will most likely need to be wired externally. If you use green wires, check whether the wire would show badly if inserted without tape. If so, it must first be taped to within 1 cm of the tip. Insert this tip carefully into the calyx in the same way as for a carnation, then gently bind the taped wire around the stem.

Gardenia and Camellia

Gardenias are sensitive to touch and seem to go brown on the slightest provocation. Even so they are wonderful flowers and are perfect for a special boutonniere, a lapel spray and, sometimes, for a bridal bouquet. To prepare a flower for wearing, first wire and tape several leaves. These are to serve as a protective collarette around the flower.

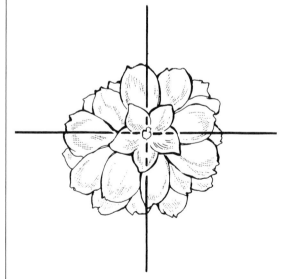

7. *Gardenias must be wired from underneath, by inserting two wires crosswise into the calyx*

Have two silver 0.46 mm wires ready, invert the flower into a bowl of water and insert the wires crosswise into the calyx (see figure 7). Holding the flower under water will prevent its being damaged by touch. Very carefully pull the two legs of wire down parallel to the stem, but not too close at this stage. Since there are two wires inserted, you will now have four wires parallel with the stem. Bring the flower out of the water, cut the stem to about 3 cm and position the leaves around the flower. Remove any excess wires and tape the remainder all together.

Camellia, although fragile, does tolerate a certain amount of handling and it is not necessary to wire under water. It will, however, require a protective collarette of foliage, which can be self-foliage or ivy leaves, should the camellia foliage be too large.

Lilies and Alstroemeria

The mid-century hybrid lilies and alstroemeria have no calyx and one is tempted to use the hook method. This is quite suitable for a head-dress or lapel spray, but for bouquets, which are subjected to a certain amount of movement, the hook can move within the flowers and sometimes break off petals. For lilies to be used in bouquets, the two-wire method is more practical.

Alstroemeria has a very solid seed box just below the flower and this is the perfect attachment point for the wire. Either drive it right through and pull each piece down parallel to the stem, or wire as for carnation. This is a very lovely flower, but it is extremely brittle and so needs to be handled with care.

UNIT BUILDING

This involves taping materials, that have already been wired and taped, to a support wire or backbone so that several pieces of material can be inserted into a design on one

UNIT MOUNTED ON 0.90 MM WIRE

8. *Unit building by adding individually wired flowers along a 0.90 mm wire*

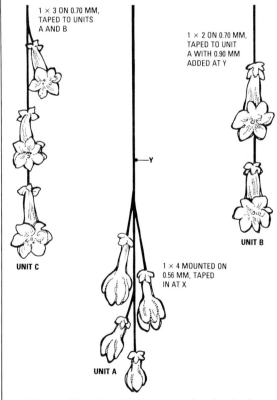

1 × 3 ON 0.70 MM, TAPED TO UNITS A AND B

1 × 2 ON 0.70 MM, TAPED TO UNIT A WITH 0.90 MM ADDED AT Y

UNIT B

UNIT C

1 × 4 MOUNTED ON 0.56 MM, TAPED IN AT X

UNIT A

9. *Unit building by adding groups already wired together*

wire. The units will describe the shape of the design and usually have lighter material at the tip, increasing in visual and actual weight towards the heart of the design. The first support wire will be relatively light, therefore, the next one heavier, and so on. One must continually test the weight, making sure that no unit becomes head-heavy. When the design is finally assembled every piece of material must appear to have originated from the very heart of the design and each unit should be assembled accordingly (see figures 8 and 9). It is not easy to decide exactly how much material should be put on one unit, but it is always easier to put less on each unit, rather than more. After all, another unit can always be added.

Providing that all material is as fresh as possible, that it has been wired and taped in the shortest possible time and then stored away out of draughts, your designs should look good and last well, for it is surprising how tolerant most flower and foliage material is to being removed from the parent plant, wired and taped and assembled into designs.

5

DESIGN AND COLOUR

Traditional British-style floristry and flower arranging consists of two basic design concepts: the three-point facing or radial arrangement and the all-round design, which is based on three, five or seven lines, plus a central perpendicular.

The word design means a plan. Therefore it is logical to expect that the plan intended by the florist or designer should be instantly recognisable by the beholder. Every flower has its own shape, size, texture and colour and this will be integrated into the finished effect.

But as well as visible shape, colour and volume, there has to be a recognisable bone structure. When planning a design it is interesting to place a line diagram over the main design to check whether the 'bones' of the arrangement, that is, the original guidelines, are in correct placement (see figure 10).

Whatever the design, outline, shape or dimension, it should be possible to define a point of origin in the finished arrangement. All materials will appear to lead in and away from a particular point. This need not necessarily be the centre of the arrangement, but it is the area from which the movement of the design is controlled. If a design has no 'heart', or 'focal point', it has no rhythm.

10. *The guidelines for a basic three-point facing design*

FIXING THE FOAM

It is vital that the design base is completely firm. The foam can be impaled on a prong which has been fixed to the base with Oasis-fix. Both container and prong, also your hands, must be quite dry, otherwise the fix will not adhere in the first instance. But once firmly in place, it will tolerate any amount of water. However, if the design is to be transported, the foam should also be firmly attached with Oasis-tape or Sellotape. Again, these tapes will not adhere if the surface of the container is damp. Sellotape is very reliable, providing you take a long enough piece to wind firmly around and fix to itself. Pull really hard so that the tape stretches as much as possible.

Never begin designing until you are satisfied that the foam is completely firm. Oasis-fix does not adhere to glass or to a very highly glazed surface. To ensure that the foam stays firmly in place, fold a paper tissue to a small square and place beneath the foam block before taping it around. The paper will act as a 'skid-mat' and the block will not move.

Add a little water to the container at this stage. You will have to drain it out again before transportation, but it ensures that the foam does not dehydrate while you are working.

Mask the foam by partially covering it with foliage or moss or a little of both. It is far quicker to mask at the beginning of an arrangement than trying to add it between the main line flowers. For a large design, such as that in Plate 6, the base must be very carefully prepared, having already chosen as capacious a container as possible, so that there is plenty of water for the large amount of material. Ideally use Jumbo-Oasis for all large designs as it will support huge branches and heavy-stemmed flowers, but if none is handy, two or three blocks of regular foam will be adequate. One needs a large-bladed knife to cut Jumbo-Oasis which has a texture that is reassuringly solid.

However, if you are using the regular brick-shaped foam, prepare the container by first, putting a block or part of one into the container to act as a platform. Next, insert a smaller block of foam on one side to act as the base for backing foliage (this is

only necessary for a facing design). Then place a second block of foam on top of the platform. This block should be slightly smaller than the first one. Place two pieces of stick or stem on top at the edge of the block, one each side (see figure 11). Pass tape over the stems and fix very firmly. The stem will prevent the tape from biting into the foam and thus diminishing some of its strength.

Check that this second block of foam is completely firm and, if not, add a second length of tape. A base prepared in this fashion will support a design at least 1½ m high.

Mask the base, having first added some water to the container. Do not, however, use large woody stems as they will take up too much foam base, leaving not enough space for the flower stems.

THREE-POINT RADIAL FACING DESIGN

This is developed from one strong perpendicular line, plus two laterals which, in outline, form an implied triangle (see figure 10). It may be of any height or width, according to where the design is to be placed. It may describe an isosceles triangle with the perpendicular much longer than the laterals—a very popular and pleasing shape. Alternatively, it can have a short perpendicular and long laterals—a design very suitable for a buffet table. For a less formal design, the outline can almost describe a right-angle triangle which results in an asymmetrical arrangement.

To begin the design, insert the first perpendicular as far back in the foam as possible. Insert two more, at varying heights and as near the first insert as convenient. These two other lines will, so to speak, emphasise your first line and thus strengthen it visually.

The first two laterals should be inserted approximately in line with where the first

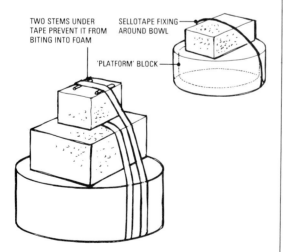

TWO STEMS UNDER TAPE PREVENT IT FROM BITING INTO FOAM

SELLOTAPE FIXING AROUND BOWL

'PLATFORM' BLOCK

11. *Building up the foam base for a large container*

perpendicular enters the foam. Do not place them too far forward as this will diminish your design area and give the finished arrangement a pinched-up appearance.

Continue to echo your three main lines, inserting each subsequent stem as near the previous one as possible. Each must be a different length and shorter than the first three, so that every flower is seen to its best advantage and the design does not appear crowded. Some material can be cut really short so that the flowers are recessed, giving visual strength and dimension to the design.

Endeavour all the time to insert the material as far back in the foam as possible, thus keeping most of the actual weight towards the back of the block. Stems at the front should be added towards the end of the construction because otherwise it will be almost impossible to get in close and place the recessed material into position. When working with gladioli or other heavy-headed flowers, it is vital to keep most of the weight well back otherwise your arrangement is likely to fall forwards.

Plate 21 is a facing design with spray carnations set off against the cool green of eucalyptus foliage. Plate 22 is composed of spray carnations (the main line flowers) and larger carnations (the dominant material), with freesia added as emphasis to the main lines. A perpendicular facing design of garden flowers in late spring is shown in Plate 4. Loosestrife is the line and dominant flower, with two groups of *Alchemilla mollis*, self-foliage and a small quantity of fern. The facing design in Plate 6 is considerably larger than the other examples but the method of construction is identical.

ALL-ROUND DESIGN

This is exactly what the name implies—a design intended to be seen from all angles. It can be made to any dimension, the main

perpendicular being set exactly in the centre of the arrangement. The base is prepared as for a facing arrangement, the foam being cut so that about 2–3 cm is above the rim of the container. This will accommodate the lateral stems, so the height of the foam must vary with the size of the stems. Mask the base.

Decide on the height and area of the arrangement. The central perpendicular line flower will determine the height. All the laterals must have the same stem-length and this will dictate the width of the design.

Insert the central flower, which should be as straight as possible from all angles (see figure 12). Then place the first laterals equidistant around the edge of the foam. You have now described the total dimension of the design. Take a second group of laterals, all the same length as each other,

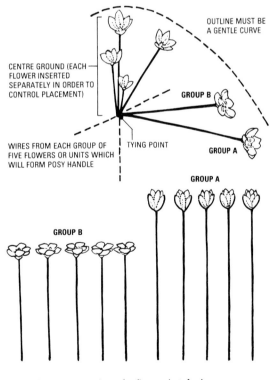

12. *The construction of a five-point design (centrepiece or posy)*

but shorter than the first group. Insert these between and slightly higher than the first group. In Plate 11 white ixia describes the strong central line while September flower (*Aster ericoides*) 'Monte Cassino' indicates the first laterals. A layer of 'Harlekijn' spray chrysanthemum and cornflower is added, plus some alstroemeria, which is inserted free-style where it seems necessary.

Once the basic shape is established, add a few more flowers and pieces of decorative foliage. While this type of design should appear to be the same from every angle, to make it too uniform would be visually very boring. The basket arrangement in Plate 8 was constructed on the same basis. When adding more layers after the main lines have been established do not crowd the flowers, since there should always be a certain amount of air space between each one.

PARALLEL FORM

Plates 2 and 15 are examples of simple parallel form, which can be both perpendicular and lateral. Unlike the radial and all-round concepts, both of which should have an apparently central heart, parallel form has several points of origin. The way loosestrife grows is a perfect example of this. On the other hand a chlorophytum plant is an example of an all-round design, its graceful foliage springing from one central point of origin.

Parallel form is particularly suited to strong straight-stemmed materials but, for maximum effect, the environment should also be suitable for this somewhat regimented style. Strangely enough, it can look wonderful in a church, especially on a wide windowsill but I do not visualise it in a country cottage with beams and chintz covers. That, however, is a purely personal view, and in spite of this, parallel form is a most appealing design concept. It is usually viewed from any angle and the materials are grouped with spaces between, so that one

can also look down and through the design. The foam can be masked with foliage, moss, stones, tiny plants or short-stemmed flowers. This is sometimes known as 'paving' or 'carpeting'.

Furthermore, it is a refreshing change from the traditional English-style radial facing and all-round designs. Certain types of flowers are especially suitable—liatris, allium, roses, delphinium, for example, although any material with a reliable straight stem can be used. The arrangement can be based in a square or oblong container, as in Plate 2, or it can be in an oval or circular base, as in Plate 20. The foam should reach just to the edge of the container, not above the rim. Each stem has to be driven in firmly and decisively for the foam is not very deep. No material is set at an angle, which imparts a very natural appearance to the design.

BIEDERMEIER

This is a design form very similar to the English Edwardian posy, which can be made either in the hand or arranged in a container. The outline is circular while the profile is very often a gentle dome-shape although sometimes it can be exaggerated to pyramid form. The flowers are set fairly closely, though not so close as in a Victorian posy. They can be placed in concentric circles of varying colours and forms, or they may be inserted more or less free-style, providing the form and outline is maintained. The outside edge is usually defined with foliage. The Biedermeier is very suited to dried flowers which should be put in in small groups for maximum effect.

PILLOW STYLE

The design should be based in a shallow dish, which may or may not have a small stem. The base is prepared with foam, cut according to the proposed size of the design and the size of the stems. Parts of the foam are masked with groups of flowers and/or berries. Small plants such as echeveria can be placed in 'terrace' style with one piece of material rising directly above another of the same sort, and closely packed (e.g. Plate 20).

The arrangement may be either front facing or with an all-round aspect. The main line flowers, the dominant material, are inserted centrally. One set of laterals is inserted at an acute angle; the second group at almost a right angle to the dominant stems. Another group is introduced towards the front of the design. The grouping of the base masking materials emphasises the heart of the design. The dominant perpendicular line provides elegance while the laterals are responsible for exciting movement and rhythm. This is a ·very satisfying design style which adapts well to almost any material at any season of the year.

DECORATIVE DESIGN

This means that any material thought relevant to the arrangement can be used, whether in its natural season or not. It gives the arranger complete freedom in both choice and use of materials. So long as it is in keeping with the design concept, flowers may be placed higher or lower in relation to others of different varieties. It therefore follows that long-stemmed flowers may sometimes be cut quite short, and those that grow naturally tall and straight, gladioli and iris, for example, may be placed in the lateral.

VEGETATIVE DESIGN

Materials must be used in their natural seasons only and should be placed in the design according to how they grow naturally. An iris must not be cut down so that the bloom is below that of a tulip. A gladiolus may not be set in the lateral position, nor would chrysanthemums and roses be con-

sidered compatible, even though both these flowers are available from the florist at the same time.

Pure vegetative design presents many challenges and fascinating problems for the designer. But the results are intriguing and, obviously, emminently natural in appearance.

MAKING THE MOST OF COLOUR

Colour is one of the most exciting wonders of the world. It is, in fact, vital to everyone's lifestyle and to their well-being. Our actions, thoughts and reactions are all influenced by colour, even though it may be subconscious. It affects our choice of garments, our furnishings, our food and is ever-present, naturally, in our gardens and flower shops.

But the practicalities of colour in relation to flowers are somewhat elusive, for petals are living tissue which is constantly changing. Thus, the 'rules' of colour-blending should only be loosely applied and frequently only in a negative sense.

In order to understand colour relationships, the colour 'wheel' has been devised. Certain colours are pleasing together, they are natural complements and this is found not only on the colour wheel but in nature. For instance, most blue iris have a bright yellow splash on each petal; the strelitzia has orange and blue bracts springing from a green sheath; both perfect examples of *complementary* colour harmony. There are two more colour-use definitions that apply to flower design, and, of course, to other fields as well. One is the arrangement of one colour known as *monochromatic*: this does not have to be one precise colour but may be tones—lighter or darker—of the chosen colour. The other is *analogous* or *adjacent* colour harmony. This is composed of colours close to one another on the colour wheel, consisting of one primary colour and 'spilling over' to the next colour, which will be a secondary colour. Other possible combinations are *triadic* (composed of three colours equidistant on the wheel) and *split-complementary*, where both colours either side of the true complementary colour are used. Figure 13 illustrates how the colour wheel is tri-sected by the three primary colours, the spaces between being occupied by secondary colours.

The following table may also help to assess the comparative impact of different colours of flowers in a design. It is worked out on the basis of how many flowers of each colour are required to achieve impact, assuming that the maximum number of flowers of each colour is ten.

Yellow	3
Red	6
Blue	8
Orange	4
Violet	9
Green	6

From this it can be seen that yellow has the most far-reaching impact and that violet has the least. It does not, however, take into consideration the effect of artificial light on the subject. This can be quite a factor, particularly in an hotel, theatre or church. But it does imply which colours are outgoing ones and which are the receding ones.

Obviously the professional florist has to work within technical convictions but the

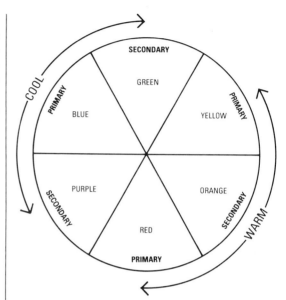

13. *The colour wheel: each primary colour is opposite a secondary colour which complements it. Colours opposite each other on the wheel provide maximum contrast.*

client must be satisfied with the result. If the two do not coincide, then professional convictions must take a back seat.

The National Association of Flower Arrangement Societies of Great Britain have published an excellent guide to colour theory which can be purchased from their headquarters at 21 Denbigh Street, London SW1V 2HF, telephone 01-838-5145.

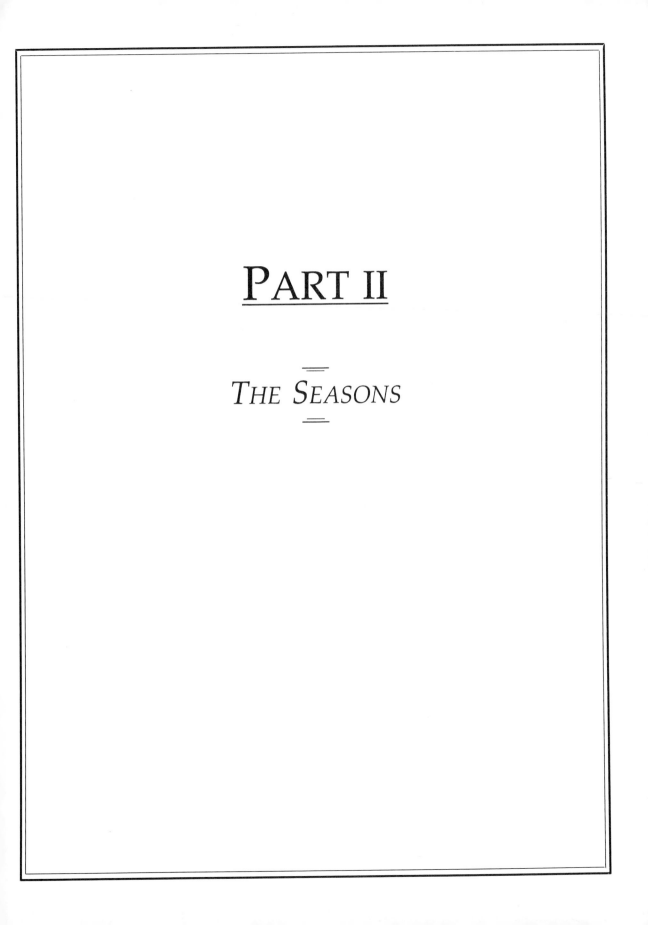

PART II

THE SEASONS

SPRING

6

FLOWERS FOR SPRING DESIGNS

Early in spring, and still technically in winter, snowdrops and wild daffodils emerge through the cold earth, sometimes in spite of a thin carpet of snow. Primroses, winter aconites and wood anemones, followed by cowslips and bluebells, add to the springtime bounty. It is certainly not warmth that tempts them, but the gradually increasing light level.

But pleasure in the first snowdrops need not be confined to country dwellers, for bunches reach the flower shops, so that everyone can have a foretaste of spring. Without doubt, they really encourage us to look forward to the richness that warmer days will bring.

Garden shrubs, also, react cheerfully to the gradually increasing light value; one of the earliest of all is *Hamamelis mollis*, whose slender deep yellow fingers uncurl on bare branches. Winter jasmine, too, offers a profusion of bright yellow flowers, sometimes even before Christmas. And for colour variation (complementary colour harmony in relation to the yellow flowers) purple *Iris stylosa* is also an 'early-riser'.

Arranging spring flowers can take very little time, given the right tools and a suitable container. Freesias, with slender pale green stems, are lovely when placed in a slender crystal vase, for the stems are almost as decorative as the flowers. Anemones, too, need very little arranging and look appealing both in crystal or pottery. Violets, also, only require a container deep enough to accommodate their stems so that the flowers, surrounded by a collarette of foliage, spread gently from the narrow neck of the vase. Give them an overhead misting with a fine spray and they should last a few days longer. In the wild, they grow in shady places so they appreciate a little artificial rain now and again.

Daffodils, synonymous with spring, should be picked when just showing colour and kept away from strong light to avoid their opening too quickly.

Tulips are known to be rather wayward in their habit of curving in various directions after having been arranged. This movement cannot be completely limited, even by judicious wiring, for a tulip will reach towards any light source and thus 'grow' beyond the confining wire. However, if they are conditioned in Chrysal solution for at least several hours before being arranged, the stems will most likely adopt their ultimate shape. The tulips in Plate 1 had been conditioned for 24 hours in a situation well away from direct light so that many of the stems were straight. Those that were determined to curve were used to describe the outline of the design. It is more positive to use an upward curve rather than turning the flower so that it droops downward.

This design is based in well-soaked foam set firmly into a simple plastic bowl. It is a simple three-point facing design with an asymmetrical bias. Very little extra foliage is necessary because each flower has its own lovely pale green crisp leaves. A few bergenia leaves contribute variation in colour and shape, and by virtue of their size, give an added strength to the base of the arrangement. This is a very good-natured plant, growing in almost any situation except extreme shade. The leaves (commonly known as elephants' ears, for obvious reason) remain all winter long, while quite early in the year the plant produces short spikes of bright pink flowers.

Hyacinths are an essential part of the early spring scene. They can easily be grown at home by buying bulbs specially prepared to flower at Christmas. Plant them in moist bulb fibre and put the container away in the dark. Check on them every few weeks and if the fibre is dry, give a little water. When the pale shoot emerges, bring into the light and water more frequently. Once the flower bud is showing, take care to water only the fibre since moisture collected at the base of the bud may cause the flower to rot.

Another intriguing method of growing a hyacinth is by placing it in a tall wine glass or proper hyacinth glass full of water. It is fascinating to watch the roots reaching down into the water once the bulb begins to grow after spending a few weeks in the dark. Growing a hyacinth or daffodil is quite a popular competition for school children who are usually given the bulb with growing instructions. There is great consternation, as one might imagine, if parents or child forget to water the poor plant and as the day of adjudication approaches, a panic visit to a florist's is not unknown!

Iris is another splendid long-stemmed flower that really belongs to late spring and early summer, but which is now produced almost all year round. Even so, this does not diminish one's delight in such stately flowers. They add colour and shape to any design, their natural foliage with silvery reverse is particularly attractive, while their form seems especially appropriate to parallel design (see Plate 2). Iris can, of course, be included in mixed traditional radial designs, but since their vase life is not so long as some other flowers, it may be more rewarding to arrange them with flowers of similar vase life—tulips, for example.

Camellias are grown in Britain by many keen gardeners and it is most satisfying to be able to include home-grown blooms in arrangements or to cut one for a lapel spray. Frances Perry reports that the first plants grown in England flowered in Essex in 1739. But it seems they were killed with kindness since the whole stock died and it was deduced that they were given too much heat. Fortunately, they were reintroduced by a member of the East India Company in 1792 when it was realised that they were tolerant of the British climate in certain areas and did not really need to be kept in a greenhouse at all.

Towards the end of May the invasive loosestrife (*Lysimachia vulgaris*) is at its best. Plate 4 shows facing arrangement in its natural form, that is, straight perpendicular. Loosestrife conveniently provides its own decorative foliage, so that little else is needed except to introduce another form and texture. Some sprays of early alchemilla inserted in the lateral, and some garden fern (*Asplenium*), give a certain amount of width to the arrangement. It may seem ungrateful to refer to loosestrife as invasive, but it can, in fact, take charge in the border if not checked.

Plate 5 is a very simple example of the three-point radial facing design which uses late spring flowers. The main central stem of white sweet pea is placed first, then the shorter lateral stem followed by the far longer curved one. These three 'signal' lines define the extremities of the arrangement. Sweet peas are wonderful flowers to arrange as the ones from the garden usually offer both curved and straight stems. Those that are grown commercially tend to have long straight stems—elegant but not so interesting from the point of view of the flower arranger.

Having established these three main lines, they are then emphasised by other similar lines, each one being somewhat shorter than the last one inserted. The scarlet sweet peas were the next group to be placed and, finally, the pink ones. The *Asparagus sprengeri* foliage was added afterwards, with the echeveria rosette right in the centre front to give visual strength to the arrangement. This is a very simple design which relies on exploiting the natural curve of each stem.

For a completely different effect, use liatris as the outline flower, with carnations and/or spray carnations as the secondary flowers; again an essentially simple combination of flower form (straight and pointed) with round flowers towards the centre.

Some flowers produce the strongest impact when used by themselves. A few stems of lilac in one colour, for example, look really opulent. Be sure to take off the foliage, then condition the stems in warm water before arranging.

To mask the foam some of the following is useful early in the year, though not all is available from the flower shop: laurel, *Eleagnus*, *Hebe* (veronica), *Ruscus*, *Asparagus*, leather leaf, *Eucalyptus*, *Buxus* (box), *Camellia*, *Helleborus foetidus* and *Viburnum tinus*. If all else fails, one can sometimes 'trim' a well-grown ivy or *Philodendron* for a special design.

Making a Spring Garden

Ingredients required are: a cork or wood base, a small container to hold soaked foam, a small block of dry foam, some shapely twigs or branches for height—catkins, sticky buds or curly willow, some green moss and/or reindeer moss (this can be obtained from the flower shop) and a few early spring flowers—a bunch of violets, a few snowdrops, aconites, primroses or muscari (grape hyacinths).

Attach the soaked foam to the small container by means of a plastic Oasis prong or just fix it firmly with Sellotape. Decide on the position of the branches, presumably towards the back of the arrangement, then fix the block of dry foam in this position, using either a glue gun or some reliable adhesive.

Attach the container and soaked foam to the base also with the glue gun or adhesive. Make a few small wire hairpins and fix the moss to both foam blocks so that it appears as natural as possible.

Grape hyacinths or a few bluebells will provide a transition between the height of the twigs or branches and the lower level of any smaller flowers chosen. The soft stem ends will probably not drive into the soaked foam very easily, so make a small spray of several flowers, bind them together with wool and attach to a short orange stick with Sellotape or another strand of wool. Drive the stick into the foam so that the stem ends of all the flowers are in contact with the foam, and, of course, neatly appearing to grow from the moss. Do the same with any other small flowers available. Keep flowers and moss fresh by misting overhead from time to time. The branches, foam bases and moss will form the basis of several different types of arrangement as the season advances. After a few early snowdrops, some short-stemmed anemones will provide different colour interest.

The type of cork base in Plate 4 would be suitable for a fairly small design of just a few branches and one little group of flowers.

7

WILD FLOWERS

Many of us can remember being enchanted by wild flowers as children. In spring there were bluebells growing in profusion as well as primroses, milkmaids and violets. But after being carried home the flowers soon wilted and lost the shining appearance they had had when growing. However, if they are put into water immediately after being gathered, and are left in the open air for several hours to condition, they will last for several days. One florist I know always carries several buckets with a little water in his car so that when he gathers wild flowers they can be put directly into water.

Until recently in Britain, all wild flowers were fighting a losing battle, for not only were the flowers being picked, but roots were dug up and some British wild flowers were seriously in danger of extinction. Cowslips, in particular, were becoming very rare, but now in some areas they are returning in glorious profusion. The plants should not be dug up for transplanting since they have extremely deep roots. Just save the seed as it ripens and scatter it casually. Within a year or so there will be another wonderful cowslip patch.

Foxgloves (*Digitalis*) grow generously in all kinds of situations. In fact, they multiple so merrily that they could soon take charge of a small garden if not checked. Plate 6 shows a casual arrangement of self-sown garden foxgloves with a seed head from the previous season added to give contrast both in colour and texture. Foxgloves dry very easily and are lovely for arrangements as well as being wired for addition to bouquets and lapel sprays.

Plate 8 shows a basket of mixed late spring wild flowers conditioned in flower food solution and left in the open air for two days before being arranged. As an experiment the basket was left outside and the flowers lasted for a further five days, though their vase life indoors would probably be only three to four days.

Early spring foliage such as wild arum should be completely submerged in water for several hours, after which it can be arranged and will last very well. At bluebell time it is tempting to cut beech foliage, but it is too early in the year and the pale green leaves do not survive. The same applies to most wild and garden foliage of deciduous trees and shrubs. Make certain they are mature before cutting them, however appealing the new growth is.

The potato produces very beautiful flowers which are delightful to use in vase arrangements. It is not, of course, strictly a wild flower, but neither is it grown for its flowers alone. Well conditioned, it has a satisfying vase life of at least five days.

Wild clematis (*Clematis vitalba*) is also known as travellers' joy or, later in the year, old man's beard, when the mass of greenish-white flowers develop into a tuft of curly white plumes. The flowers exude a perfume similar to vanilla and sprays of clematis are very lovely when included in a large display design. In the autumn, the plumes should be cut before they develop completely, otherwise they will shed, although this can be restricted by spraying with Clear-Life or a non-perfumed hair-spray.

One August, being commissioned to decorate a city church which was rather short of funds, we used huge branches of wild clematis as well as its long, twisted woody stems, which are extremely decorative in themselves. This very effectively supplemented the more traditional flowers usually used in church decoration and, against the dark wood, brought a breath of the country into the centre of London.

Wild honeysuckle (*Lonicera periclymenum*) is another hedge flower that has a special appeal. Samuel Pepys, the seventeenth-century diarist, called it 'the trumpet flower whose bugles blow scent instead of sound'. Too true, for on a warm sunny day in June one can smell honeysuckle in the hedgerows almost before one sees it. Unfortunately, it only has a very short vase life, but it is still worth the trouble of cutting and conditioning a little, if only to savour the perfume. Later in the year, it produces bright red berries which are also very decorative.

Cuckoo flower (*Cardamine pratensis*) is a very appealing delicate-looking pinkish mauve flower which can be found in damp fields and near streams. So far as I know, it is a very local flower, nothing like so ubiquitous as wild parsley or honeysuckle. Cut it sparingly if you do find it, condition it well and it will last for several days.

Wild arum is also known as lords and ladies and Jack-in-the-pulpit. The foliage appears first, some plain green, but other varieties have black-spotted leaves, which are very decorative. The flower, however, is not particularly decorative away from its natural environment. Later in the year the spathe develops bright red berries which are very poisonous. In spite of this, however, it is nice to know that the plant has, or rather had, some domestic use, for it seems that the roots contain a high starch content. They were used in Elizabethan times for stiffening the pleated linen ruffs that were then so fashionable. If the foliage is submerged for several hours, it is excellent for small decorative designs.

Queen Anne's lace or wild parsley, of which there appear to be at least eight different types, will last very well for decoration if cut and put into water immediately. But they must be cut and not picked for one type, hemlock, is very poisonous. Presumably no one would think of eating it but the stems, if picked instead of being cut with a sharp knife, exude poison which might be transmitted to the mouth. It has, in fact, been known to cause unpleasant rashes and somnolence. There is another variety called fools parsley (*Aethusa cynapium*) which is lethal to animals and also very dangerous to people.

Yet another type, the giant hogweed (*Heracleum mantagazzianum*) which grows to a height of 3–4 m, is used by Danish florists in decorative design. Attending an international design seminar many years ago, I assumed that this material had been shipped in for our special benefit, for it was difficult to visualise such monsters being part of the regular commercial scene. But, on visiting the wholesale market, there it was, in giant bunches of several stems. The Danes regard wild flowers as part of their valid design material, even in the city shops. A traditional Danish bridal bouquet should always contain at least one variety of wild flower. Now some wild material is being pre-treated at source to prolong the vase life, so it is probable that more and more of this lovely material will become available to people who are not lucky enough to have access to the countryside.

For more information on native wild flowers, *The Field Guide to the Wild Flowers of Britain*, published by Reader's Digest, contains a wealth of information, together with colour illustrations of every plant, including pictures of individual florets, buds, berries, seeds and foliage.

8

SPECIAL OCCASIONS IN SPRING

ST VALENTINE'S DAY

Whilst 14 February is still technically in the winter season, from the flower angle there is more than a hint of spring in the air. Just how St Valentine came to be connected with this particular day is open to conjecture for what little information there is about him is both charming and decidedly grisly.

He was beheaded on 14 February, though for what crime—if any—is not recorded. This is also the date on which the birds are reputed to select their mates for the coming season. Thus it could be that because of an accident of date, St Valentine was chosen to be the patron saint of lovers.

It was in Victorian times that sending cards became high fashion and apparently the Queen herself was so taken with the idea that she sent some hundreds of 'Valentines' every year. These were quite elaborate in design, with pictures of flowers or even with pressed flowers, and sometimes edged with lace. Ladies of leisure spent many hours devising these saccharine tokens while others were produced commercially. Obviously the royal enthusiasm encouraged the industry, though it is likely that few of the pictures and verses would be acceptable today.

Now both cards and gifts of flowers are in vogue. The flowers vary from attractive spring flower presentation bouquets to a single red rose. The sentiment once expressed by the Dutch Bulb Growers' Association seems appropriate here—'one flower is worth a thousand words: think what a bunch will do .

In this scientific and computerised world, it is encouraging to realise that sentiment is still strong enough for St Valentine's Day to be celebrated throughout Europe and with tremendous enthusiasm in America where cards and gifts are on display immediately after New Year. Red roses are in most popular demand and gifts vary from lavish gift-wrapped bouquets to the single rose in cellophane or in a box trimmed with ribbon.

MOTHERING SUNDAY

This falls three weeks before Easter and consequently varies from year to year according to that date. Most other countries celebrate Mother's Day on a specific date which is not tied in with the church festival.

Flowering plants which are available as gifts at this time include cyclamen, azalea, polyanthus, the charming miniature cyclamen and the wonderfully perfumed jasmine which is usually at its best in March and April. Once it has finished flowering it can be planted in the garden for it is relatively hardy and usually survives the winter. Polyanthus, too, can be planted in a shady situation and should flower and increase year after year. Cyclamen and azalea, once they have finished flowering, should be stored outside in the pot, preferably sunk into the soil in the shade, but not where trees will drip on them. The plants need to rest for a few months and can be brought indoors again at the beginning of October.

A planted bowl, dish garden or basket is fun to make and lovely to receive. Plate 33 shows a formal example of a planted bowl

PLATE 1

*An asymmetrical traditional radial design, in a deep
ridged plastic bowl, of all tulips with tulip and
bergenia foliage*

*(Above) An arrangement in a shallow basket of tulips and iris, showing
parallel form both in the perpendicular and horizontal. The base is
emphasised with echevaria rosettes. (Below) Oncidiums in a more
modest setting for a coffee table design in a Poole pottery bowl, with
lateral sprays of cotoneaster foliage*

PLATE 4

*Loosestrife and alchemilla with garden fern
(asplenium), in a hand-made deep blue square
container set on a cork base*

PLATE 5

*Mixed sweet peas with sprengeri fern and
echevaria rosettes*

PLATE 6

Self-sown foxgloves with one stem dried from the previous season. This stem is wrapped with plastic to insulate it from the water. The arrangement is emphasised with single leaves of incense poplar (Populus candicans). *This foliage must be very well-conditioned before being arranged.*

PLATE 7

*A yellow and white late spring basket, based on the
five-point method, including freesia, alstroemeria,
solidaster, roses and antirrhinum*

PLATE 8

Mixed wild flowers and grasses in a rustic container

PLATE 9

*Bouquet for a spring wedding composed of Lilium 'Rosita',
pink alstroemeria, spray roses and September flower*

but, by adding one or two stems of fresh flowers, perhaps freesia or roses, or even three lovely daffodils, the effect would be transformed. The flower stems should be inserted into a glass tube which can be driven into the soil. Most florists have plenty of these tubes as imported flowers like anthurium, gerbera and orchids are usually shipped in them.

Polyanthus planted into a bowl are very colourful and easy to maintain. Add a small fern, if there is sufficient space, and this will provide some height and variation in texture. Several saintpaulias (African violets) massed in a bowl look really lovely, whether all of one colour or mixed tints. A larger bowl could contain, two foliage plants, such as ficus and ivy, a flowering plant like a polyanthus and a hyacinth.

Make every effort not to disturb the root ball of each plant. Try to extract it from its pot in one piece so that the roots remain relatively undamaged. To do this, place two fingers across the top of the pot either side of the plant, grasping the pot in the same hand. Turn the pot upside-down and hold with the other hand. Knock the edge of the pot sharply against the potting bench and the whole plant should come out intact into the hand. Finish the surface of the soil with either moss or small pebbles. Add a ribbon bow, too, if you wish.

A quick and attractive gift can be made with a basket. Line it with some plastic and then arrange some pot plants in it. Cover the pots with moss so that they are not visible.

Flowers suitable for a gift basket for Mothers' Day include daffodils, tulips, freesia, chincherinchee, muscari and a few stems of nerine. Wallflowers (*Cheiranthus*) could be well recessed in the arrangement, thus adding perfume and colour to the gift.

For the florist this is the busiest time of the year and plans have to be formulated well in advance to cope with the extra volume of work. It can be quite daunting for even the most professional of florists, for few of us have second sight to divine how many people will buy flowers and what will be their spending level.

The public is becoming more aware of flowers and they recognise good quality. Flowering plants make a lovely shop display and usually last longer than many cut flowers. So, to be sure of an enticing display for this special weekend, carry a good selection of flowering plants at all price levels.

There will, of course, be a gradual build-up of firm orders on your file, but you must also cater for the impulse buyer. No one can tell accurately how many of these there will be, nor how much each will spend, for all kinds of outside influences could affect the volume of customers. For example, very bad weather would keep people indoors.

There are a few guidelines that may help the buyer. Flowers with a limited potential vase life should be bought with caution for, if they are not all sold, they would be obvious waste. These include daffodils, narcissus, iris tulips and some roses. Conversely, carnations, spray carnations, spray chrysanthemums and Singapore orchids have a long vase life and make a firm back-up to the spring flowers and any unusual 'specials' you may care to stock.

Most impulse buyers want a bouquet immediately and do not want to choose flowers and then wait to have them gift-wrapped. So it helps to have some bouquets already prepared to various price levels. This engenders confidence, particularly in people who are not in the habit of regular flower-buying: they can see at a glance what they will get for a given price.

A selection of ribbon bows should be prepared well ahead (see chapter 11). Store them in large see-through cellophane bags, very loosely, so they do not crush. Show any extra temporary help how to make the bows, so that they can keep the production line going. Check well in advance that you have enough of all the sundries you will require to make up gift bouquets such as cards and envelopes, efficient staplers, Sellotape, ribbons and order pads.

It is usually acceptable for most gifts to be delivered on the Saturday before Mothering Sunday, though some florists also like to deliver on the Sunday. Whatever your chosen policy, spend time planning the routes on the Friday, so that your drivers are reasonably organised.

When taking orders, try to get as much information as possible on the location. Just the name of a house and an area can be extremely frustrating, for house-names are not always clearly displayed. Provide the driver with some 'attempted delivery' cards, so that if no one is at home, and it is not possible to leave the gift with a neighbour, a card can be left asking the recipient to contact the shop. In many cases, the flowers are collected which saves the florist a second delivery.

EASTER

This is the season to enjoy traditional spring flowers to the maximum for some will soon be gone for yet another year. Daffodils, snowdrops, tulips, anemones, hyacinths, narcissus and ranunculus are certainly not yet seen all-year-round. Flowers in country churches at this time look wonderfully cheerful, for many arrangers prefer garden-grown flowers to the more formal lily arrangements. Prunus, forsythia, snowball tree and lilac, arranged with a few garden-grown lilies or iris, are the very essence of springtime.

For the florist, white lilies (both arums and *Lilium longiflorum*) will be in heavy demand at Easter, particularly from church groups. It is advisable to place a pilot order with your wholesaler so as to be sure of your basic quantity. You can add to this as other orders arrive.

Easter Baskets

Gift baskets for Easter, like spring gardens, can be fun to design. Your choice of garden and wild flowers will, of course, depend on how early Easter falls in the year and the prevailing weather at the time. Look for the white or yellow deadnettle which, if defoliated, is very decorative. Daffodils are synonymous with Easter and the wild variety grows in some areas in glorious profusion. Take care when gathering them not to pull up the bulb.

If you prefer a slightly more sophisticated design, mixed freesias with a few lovely heads of hyacinth would make a beautifully perfumed Easter gift. To secure the hyacinth stems in the foam, carefully insert an orange stick into the stem. Hold the flower stem at the base and gently push the orange stick into the foam till the stem end is resting on the damp block.

9

WEDDINGS

For springtime weddings, the choice of flowers is wonderfully rich. Apart from roses and carnations, available more or less all year round, there is the possibility of elegant line bouquets of iris and posies of freesias.

Earlier in the season there is the simple appeal of a snowdrop bouquet. This is easily made providing you have enough flowers: for an average-sized posy about 200 stems are required. Collect the flowers into small bunches and secure each bunch with wool. Keep the stems as long as possible and when each little bunch is secure, place in water. The wool will also soak up some water and help to keep the flowers fresh. Also needed will be some long-stemmed mature ivy leaves already clean and conditioned. Collect the flower bunches into one larger bunch and edge with the leaves. Bind all together firmly but gently with another strand of wool. Prepare some ribbon trimmings if required. Leave the posy in water until it is wanted, then gently dry the stems and cover the wool bind with ribbon. The effect will be of a huge bunch of snowdrops just picked and tied with ribbon.

Plate 9 shows a line bouquet for a country wedding, the main flowers are lilies ('Rosita') with tiny pink roses and the ever-popular Monte Cassino (September flower) forming a delicate lace-like edge to the design.

The colourful church pedestal in Plate 10 also includes *Lilium* 'Rosita' with a selection of other late spring flowers, including eremurus, delphinium, stock and moluccella which were chosen for their length of stem and colour.

ORGANISATION

Much of the organisation for this special day falls on the bride and her family. The longer ahead plans can be finalised, the better as reception halls, caterers, churches and even vicars get booked well in advance.

Weddings are a highly challenging part of the professional florist's work. They involve technical ability, techniques of estimating quantities, together with impeccable organisation.

Discuss as much as possible with the prospective client before being committed to a firm price. Try to identify with her ideas, the number and type of designs wanted, the kinds of flowers preferred and the projected colour scheme details. Never be manoeuvred into making a snap decision on cost.

The most professional approach is to begin by discussing colour preferences. This will lead you to specifics of possible flower varieties. Allowing for certain seasonal limitations, the choice is usually sufficiently broad for there to be little trouble in agreeing on the final selection. The main thing is never to promise any particular item; this avoids a last-minute disappointment.

Try to discuss all the items before introducing the question of cost, unless you happen to know that the client has a very tight budget. In this case, you will have to decide between you what are the most important items and which can be cut down in price. Obviously, the bridal bouquet is paramount and it is vital that, so far as possible, the bride has exactly what she wants. After the bouquet has been agreed, the remaining items can more easily be tailored to suit the client's budget. But where the cost is not of importance it is still far more satisfactory, and more business-like, for both parties if a ceiling figure can be agreed upon, along with a marginal contingency sum to allow for possible seasonal fluctuation or any other unforeseen situation. You will, of course, need time to work out your costing, but try to produce a fair copy of the wedding order with your quotation within 48 hours. Then, assuming this is agreeable to the client, it is appropriate to ask for a deposit on the total sum.

It may be necessary, before you finalise your quotation, to visit the places to be decorated (church, reception hall or hotel, for instance) to take measurements and to make notes, including sketches if required. Never trust to memory for these vital details, for the assignment may be several months in the future.

Having assessed which flowers and foliages are necessary for each design, compile an outline buying list. The time of year and prevailing weather will have some bearing on choice. For example, in spring or summer you may have access to some wild flowers; these are rising in popularity and some are available from the wholesale market. Clarify whether the designs will be left in place or whether they are to be removed immediately after the event. If the first, then they should be based in containers with as much water capacity as possible.

There is no doubt that time spent in planning for any large-scale project, whether a wedding or other occasion, is well worth the effort and a realistic timetable should be developed from your list of items to be prepared. All this becomes second nature, as one gains more experience. Furthermore, if you work as a team, do make sure that everyone is aware of the total project. For colleagues to give the maximum help, they must understand the objective. Make sketches, with appropriate measurements, of the areas to be decorated. If several de-

signs are similar in shape and size, prepare one as a pattern so that the others can be made by someone else.

FLOWERS FOR THE BRIDE, BRIDESMAIDS AND GUESTS

A Traditional English-style Bouquet

The design is composed of various units and single flowers, assembled on the basis of an inverted three-point facing design. Like the container arrangement, it can be built either by securing the longest units first and working inwards; or from the centre outwards. Either method works well.

First prepare any ribbons required (see chapter 11), usually three butterfly bows and one multi-loop bow in narrow matching ribbon. Also prepare any ribbon trails, if needed.

Wire and tape foliage and build into units as necessary (see chapter 4). Wire and tape all flower material and put together into units. Prepare five units for the top of the design and assemble trail units in varying lengths. Mount the units on either 0.70 or 0.90 mm wires. The longer trail units can be started on 0.70 mm and the heavier wire added towards the centre. It is not necessary for the edge flowers and foliage to be supported with overly heavy wire, which would give the finished design a very stiff appearance.

Decide on length of main trail, from tip to binding point. Then add one of the five top units, placing it parallel with the trail and bind the two trails together firmly down to the end of the handle. Bend the top unit back over your hand from the central binding point, thus completing the full length of the bouquet from topmost flower to the end of the main trail. The units above the central binding point are called the returned end (see figure 14).

Next, insert the central flower. Your design now has volume as well as length. Add other units, securing them at the central

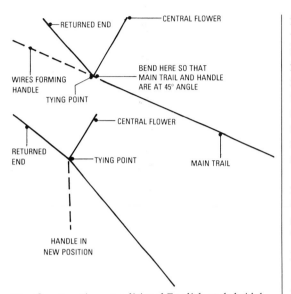

14. *Constructing a traditional English-style bridal bouquet*

tying point. Do not bend the units before you insert them. Insert them completely straight, bind firmly and then bend sharply so that the unit is completely controlled from the tying point. If necessary, insert the three ribbon bows to camouflage any 'machinery', setting them right into the heart of the bouquet.

Cut the handle to the required length and finish very carefully. Never skimp this part of the design, for the ribbon must be totally secure, no matter how much the design is handled.

Bouquets and Posies in Foam Holders

The firm of Smithers-Oasis produces several types of bouquet holder, in varying sizes, with foam that has to be soaked before use. Florists find that the flowers last far longer in these bases and also that design time can be cut down, which is a most important factor in a busy shop. However, the holders are plastic, as are the handles, and they should be covered with ribbon to make them a little more elegant.

Val Spicer Designs offers a holder which is light in both weight and design. The plastic base which supports a small ball of dry foam is available in several sizes. It is backed with white or cream tulle. The flowers survive well in dry foam providing that they are completely fresh, of top quality and have been adequately conditioned. For, assuming that the flower and stem is as full of water as possible, the dry foam clogs.the stem-end, thus holding the water in.

But these bouquet holders are by no means a substitute for basic floristry skills. One should first be proficient in constructing a bouquet or posy in the hand to understand the complications of weight and balance. The centre of a foam-based bouquet will obviously be larger than one that has been constructed on units and then bound tightly at the centre. This foam has first to be masked, as for a vase arrangement and any long trails must be wired and the wire returned into the foam base, otherwise gravity will take charge, and the trail may part company with the base.

Head-dresses

The fashion now is for rather large head-dresses, usually assembled as a circlet. They take a great deal of material and time and this must never be underestimated. Check with the bride how the design is to be worn —as a small coronet-style or as a full circlet around the largest part of the head. A young child's head is only slightly smaller than an adult's, though there is often a considerable difference in the thickness of hair and this will make a difference to the measurement.

Cut some binding wire (about 0.56 mm gauge) to the required length plus approximately an extra 8 cm. Tape the first 4 cm of wire then bend it over to form a loop and tape firmly. Continue taping along the whole length of wire. Then bend the last 4 cm back to form another loop.

Wire and tape all necessary materials, using only very short stems. This is sometimes known as a closed unit, meaning that all the material is taped to the base wire so closely that no stems are visible. If you are working to a specific flower and foliage progression, it will be necessary to lay everything ready on the workbench so that you can see how it looks and whether you will have sufficient materials. If you are working free-style still make sure that you have prepared enough of each type of bud, flower and leaf used.

Do not cut any excess wires away at the beginning, but as more material is added, the circlet may begin to feel heavy and stiff. If you are using roses which are rather heavy flowers, leave all wires in so that the finished design is not too whippy. Check for weight and rigidity about every 10 cm and continue adding materials until you reach the other loop. Then curve the circlet around so that the first piece of material overlaps the last and no join is visible.

If a ribbon finish is wanted, make one small multi-loop bow. Then pass a long piece of matching ribbon through both loops and tie them together with the bow in the centre. This is very attractive as it can be seen by the wedding guests during the ceremony. Check with the bride how lavish she would like these ribbons. Some like a cascade with the small multi-loop actually on the design; others prefer a more under-stated effect as described above.

Packing Bridal Flowers

There are special boxes available for packing, but they are somewhat expensive. Some florists levy a deposit on the box, which is returnable within a given time, but this proves time-consuming. The alternative is to cover a box (usually a flower box) with paper; either the shop's own wrapping paper or with thin wallpaper from a DIY store. It takes time but looks very attractive. Having carefully covered the outside of the box—either lid or base, not both—attach transparent paper to one side and to both ends of the box.

Put some wood shavings, polystyrene chips, or similar, into the box to make a soft bed for the designs. Cover with white tissue paper. Make a small hole in the paper through which to thread the handles of the designs so that the flowers are resting on the tissue paper. Also add more paper behind the designs where necessary, for it is vital that they all fit firmly and do not roll about in transit. Arrange the ribbon trails so that they are quite flat and smooth; if necessary, protect them with more tissue paper.

Give the designs a light top spray and seal the transparent covering to the other side of the box, so that when the designs are delivered, everyone can see them and will not be tempted to handle them before the ceremony.

A second method is to cover a box or lid as previously described. Then invert it and make a cross-cut with a sharp knife through which you can thread the bouquet handle. Lay some tissue paper between the design and the box to cushion the flowers. Seal as described above. With this method the flowers, being on top of the box and not inside, are not quite so protected, but less packing is required.

Buttonholes

There seems to be some confusion regarding the protocol surrounding the use of buttonholes. Should there be one provided for every wedding guest? Should they always be white? Should there be fern with them? The trend now is for people to have whatever they want, so it is really a matter of individual choice. But if the bridal family has had little or no experience of wedding etiquette, the florist should be able to advise on all the main points.

It is not necessary to provide buttonholes for every guest, but would be a lovely gesture if the family wishes to do so.

The flowers used need not be white, though it is customary for the bridegroom, his best man, the ushers and for the gentleman who is 'giving away' the bride to have the same colour. If the bridegroom wants something entirely different, suggest that his buttonhole is made with one of the flowers in the bride's bouquet.

Some men hate being decorated with a large flower and the florist should be sympathetic to this point of view. Suggest a single Singapore orchid, a tiny rose, a button dahlia or even a minute rosette of foliage and berries.

Whether fern is used with carnations is a personal decision. I think fern makes an already overlarge flower look overdone so, unless there is a specific request for fern or carnation grass, carnation buttonholes are always delivered without fern.

One is sometimes asked which way up the lapel spray should be worn. This is again a personal decision but it would seem logical to wear the design with the stems pointing downwards. It should be worn on whichever shoulder feels the most comfortable. Being right-handed, I find it almost impossible to pin on to the right shoulder. The spray should be pinned really high, so that the shoulderblade supports any slight weight. If the dress fabric is delicate, even the slightest extra weight may drag it and, anyway, if it is worn high, it is seen to better advantage. A well-balanced design should require only one pin to attach it across the main perpendicular, though two should be sent just in case one is mislaid.

Buttonholes, lapel sprays and headdresses, as well as the cake decoration, tend sometimes to be made by the florist as an afterthought. All one's mental energy has been expended on the bouquets and the smaller items sometimes prove to be the last straw. Time is getting short and yet it is often the case that these smaller designs take more time and patience than the larger ones. Therefore I have found it best to make all these first; spray them and pack them away ready for despatch. One pin should be

added for a gentleman's boutonnière and two for a lady's spray. Never put them loose into the despatch box; attach them to ceiling tiles in families and cover them with polythene.

Prepare any ribbon required in advance (see chapter 11). This can be stored in clear plastic bags and labelled with the bride's name and date of wedding. Foliage can be wired and taped two or three days ahead as it will keep well if sprayed and stored in plastic bags or boxes.

Before beginning work, make sure that you have all the necessary materials handy; the correct wires, split tape and a bowl of clean water, plus, of course, the foliage and flower material. If you are using guttapercha it is not necessary to split it, since it stretches to a much thinner texture. Other tapes, such as Stemtex and Floratape, should be split so that the finish of the designs is far more delicate. If you do not have a tape splitter, put the reel on a door handle, pull a length out at tension and run your shears along it. It takes so little time and the difference in finish is quite remarkable.

As you wire and tape each piece of material, place it in the bowl of water (head first). This will keep it fresh until you are ready to assemble the design. If you are making several items of more or less the same materials, prepare them all and put them in separate plastic bags. They can then be assembled later on; this method is far quicker than wiring, taping and assembling each separate item.

So that the designs all arrive looking really fresh try to wire and tape an item in one movement and then place it immediately into water. This helps to ensure that the material remains fresh-looking for the next 48 hours.

Carnation boutonnière: Cut the flower stem to about 3 cm. Insert a 0.70 mm wire through the stem and right into the flower. Push it right up so that it extends above the flower far enough for you to make a small hook. Retract the wire gently so that the hook rests within the flower. Cut the wire to about 7 cm finished length. Tape from base of stem to end of wire. Insert a pin into the calyx so that it can easily be seen (this is for attaching to the lapel).

A *single rose boutonnière* can be made for a gentleman. Begin by preparing the rose foliage, wiring two leaves together three times. Rose leaves are rather thin so wiring two together gives them an extra dimension that helps them to last longer. Place them one on top of the other not back to back. Give a twist of tape to seal the leaf stem, but there is no need to tape to the end of the wire.

Cut the rose stem down to about 3 cm. Wire internally, if possible, with 0.70 or 0.90 mm wire using the hook method. If the stem is too tough, wire it externally by inserting a 0.70 mm wire into the calyx and twisting it once around the stem. Tape the base of the stem, but not right down to the end of the wire.

Arrange the leaves around the bud, one to the back and the other two at the side and slightly curved forwards. Secure with two

15. *A single rose to be worn on a lady's lapel*

twists of fine wire. Cut wires to an approximate length of 7 cm and tape all together.

For a single rose which can be worn on a lady's lapel prepare the materials in the same way as above, but tape all the wires to the end. Assemble in the same way, but leave the four stems free. Secure just under the bud with two twists of fine wire and overbind this area with tape (see figure 15).

FLOWERS FOR DECORATION
Pew Ends
In most cases these will be removed after the ceremony so that they can either be designed in dry foam bases or on the specially-designed base called Le Klip, which needs soaking first. Le Klip will fit most pews, but it is advisable to check first to see if any adjustments are needed.

It is always best to do as much work in advance on the workbench as possible. Taking the measurements of the pew ends in advance means that they can be assembled and put in place at the last moment. They must not be too deep—two people should be able to walk comfortably side-by-side up and down the aisle.

The design technique should be similar to an inverted facing design. It will be observed from the sides and also from the top, but it is unlikely that people will look at it 'square-on' as one might look at a wall swag, for example. Therefore, insert most stems as far back as possible, so that the finished design is apparently 'growing' from the pew end and make sure that the base is masked first. The central flowers should be inserted at a very slight angle, so that they face towards the top and not directly outwards (see figure 16).

If soaked foam is used, do make sure that it has stopped dripping before you put the pew ends in place. Prepare the ribbon trimmings and add them last of all. It is not always necessary to hang designs on every pew. This can appear rather overdone in

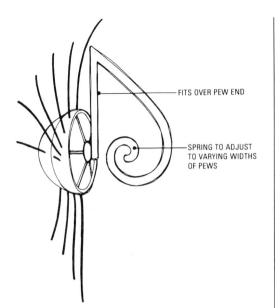

wire legs so that the design rests flat on the cake.

Some brides, however, prefer to have the flowers in a container, which may vary in style from the simple silvered plastic flute vase or little basket to a real silver container. My favourite is a Waterford glass container which looks wonderfully light and airy. Flowers in a container are arranged as for an all-round centrepiece, with a tall centre line and shorter laterals in balance with the area of the top tier of the cake. Trailing foliage or ribbons can be added if required.

This posy could also be wired and assembled in the hand, using the three- or five-point method with an exaggerated central line. When complete, try it in the container to check whether the 'handle' fits tightly

16. *Assembly of a decoration for the end of a church pew*

some churches and placing them on alternate ones is usually sufficient.

The Cake Top
Prepare the ribbon trimmings, wire and tape material, assembling three or five laterals into units. The cake top is bound together in the same way as an all-round posy, but the binding point should be kept as slender as possible. Therefore, build as much into units as possible (see figure 17). The central line should be tall and graceful so that the design appears as an elegant finish to the cake.

When all ingredients have been bound in to the central point, overbind this tiny area with tape. Turn the design over and divide the wires into three sections. Cut these 'legs' down to about 5 cm and carefully tape each one. These can also be covered with ribbon if a very special finish is required. Next bend each leg around to form a half-circle and also bend the first set of lateral units slightly towards the legs so that the binding point is not visible. Adjust these

17. *The method of securing flowers for a cake top decoration*

and whether it is the correct length, as the laterals should spray over the edge of the container and not stand proud of it. If necessary, overbind the handle with a paper tissue to make it larger, then finish with tape and ribbon.

Marquee Decoration

Most firms that supply marquees are accustomed to working in parallel with the florist and, in many instances, fixing hooks for designs are already in place. This must be checked before the work is begun for some other method of fixing may be needed. This must be planned and agreed with the firm in advance before too many nails are knocked in.

A reliable base is obviously required for the pole swags: the Grandee by Smithers-Oasis is excellent. It is very strong and will support a remarkable quantity of material.

Pass a strong wire across the base, that is to say, over the plastic container but under the foam insert. Also thread a second wire through the hole in the handle. Florists' wire will not be strong enough as the final weight of the design will be considerable. Marquee poles are usually circular, so it is also advisable to fix a large piece of double-sided adhesive to the back of the base, to prevent the design from swinging. The tape used for fixing rugs and carpets to the floor is very effective.

Do as much preparation as possible on the workbench, even to adding most of the flowers. The swags should be positioned as high as possible, so that the tip of the longest flower or foliage is about 2½ m above ground level.

The marquee is usually put in place two or three days before the event, so this will give you a chance to visit the site to make sure that you are thoroughly acquainted with the situation and any possible problems.

Although most of the design will have been done before they are put in place, take extra flowers and foliage which can be added on the spot. The visual emphasis will obviously be mainly from the base and the sides. The colour scheme will already have been agreed with the client. Try to choose flowers which are resistant to hot or windy weather—such as carnations and gladioli. Reliable foliage is also a great help for large designs. There is a firm in southern Ireland that will supply quite large branches, if ordered well in advance. They also pack boxes of smaller foliage (mainly several varieties of eucalyptus) for general design use. (For name and address see Suppliers.)

Materials used for a short-term decoration are rarely of any use afterwards and it is not usually feasible to rely on any returns. Thus the cost of the bases and the time taken to dismantle must be realistically costed in to your original quotation.

The Auto-corso

This base is really intended for decorating bridal cars, but it can be used for other designs as well. Produced by the Smithers-Oasis organisation, it consists of a block of foam encased in wide-mesh plastic. This is removable, so that the base could be used several times, if required. On the reverse is a large suction cap which adheres firmly to almost any type of surface, providing it is quite smooth. When fixing it to the car, make sure that there is not the slightest piece of grit or dust on the spot where the auto-corso is to be attached. The block measures approximately 10 cm by 8 cm and will therefore support quite a large amount of flowers and foliage. It is very effective when fixed to a mirror for party and Christmas decoration; it can also be used for wall and door swags.

The bridal limousine looks very festive with a large design attached either to the back or resting on the side of the bonnet. Obviously care must be taken to ensure that it does not impair the driver's view. The base is first soaked and then fixed firmly to the vehicle. The three-point facing technique is the best design method to use, with an extra line added from the centre towards the front of the arrangement. Providing the car is not driven at top speed, the design will stay in place. A similar one was attached to a car in Spain and the car then driven some 25 miles at about 40 mph. The design was still perfectly secure on arrival.

SUMMER

10

FLOWERS FOR SUMMER DESIGNS

Even though the reality of summer is rarely as idyllic as our dreams, we still enjoy a profusion of flowers in gardens and florist's shops. The temperature may not be as high as we would like it but even so flowers tend not to last as long as they do in winter.

It is certainly a great temptation to buy or pick flowers and flowering plants in tight bud, hoping that the buds will gently expand and so give us longer enjoyment. Unfortunately this does not always happen. Notable examples are iris, spray carnations, tulips and roses which, if harvested too early, will never reach full maturity, even with the help of nutrient solutions.

Shelf and vase life can be increased in the summer by keeping flowers and flowering plants away from direct sunlight. Never leave a gift-wrapped bouquet or plant in cellophane exposed to sun or strong light.

With warmer weather approaching many flowers in the pink, mauve and blue colour range—hydrangea, sweet pea, delphinium, larkspur, scabious and love-in-a-mist (*Nigella*) for instance—can be found in our gardens and flower shops.

One of the most lovely of the late spring/ early summer flowers are sweet peas. These are not long-lasting unless they are cut and arranged directly from the garden, for, like dahlias, they do not like being bunched and packed. So, if mixed with other longer-lasting flowers such as carnations or spray chrysanthemums, they might eventually make the design look untidy. By themselves they are truly appealing. Plate 5 shows a very simple facing design with *Asparagus*

sprengeri for foliage and a large echeveria to give central emphasis.

The all-round design shown in Plate 11 uses summer flowers together with some that are available all year round. The white ixia forming a strong central line and the original five lateral points are indicated with September flower, echoed by cornflowers alternately. The spray chrysanthemums are rather large in proportion to the whole design, and their colour also carries strong impact, so only five stems were inserted in the lateral with just three more flowers for continuity towards the centre.

Cream alstroemeria and white love-in-a-mist were inserted to modify the somewhat strident effect of the chrysanthemum. Finally some solidaster was added to introduce yet another texture and colour variation. In a plastic wood-look compote, the effect is essentially informal and cottagey.

Featuring in the pink and yellow colour groups is the tall and stately eremurus which is so wonderful for line work. Its use can be seen in Plate 10. Remember to condition eremurus for 48 hours otherwise the flower tip will not stay upright. The plants can be grown outside in Britain and require a well-drained soil with plenty of space for the roots which are very fleshy and spread out in all directions, rather like a starfish. They are advertised in some of the gardening catalogues but it can be several years before they flower.

Valuable for foliage effects at this time of the year are the spurges (*Euphorbia*). Several varieties can be cultivated, both for decoration and as ground cover including *E.*

wulfenii which is a dignified plant with bluish-green foliage and yellow bracts, growing to a height of approximately 60 cm.

ROSES

The rose is probably the best-known flower in the world and, some say, the oldest. Gerard in his Herball offers the thought that the first rose sprang from the blood of Venus, while others maintain that it was connected with the Prophet Mahommet.

The florist should buy roses from a reputable wholesaler who understands the seasonal problems. They should certainly be bought in bud, with the colour just showing, and the foliage must be strong and firm. Roses are very susceptible to both light and heat, and also to contaminants in the water. So it is vital that any containers used either for storage or display are absolutely clean.

The quickest and most effective way of cleaning any container (except precious metal) is to fill it with a weak solution or ordinary domestic bleach. Leave it for about 30 minutes, rinse thoroughly and dry.

Prepare the containers with a flower food solution, lukewarm unless the weather is very hot. Strip the lower few leaves from each stem and, using a clean sharp knife, cut the stem-end with a crisp cut. Roses for designs and shop sale need to be de-thorned; otherwise handling can be very frustrating. Thorns can be removed by hand, which is a slow process, and so they are usually cut off with scissors or sliced off with a knife. This needs care, as a ragged torn wound will allow bacteria to enter. Roses for bridal designs are usually used on far shorter stems and so do not need to be de-thorned. Garden roses usually have more thorns than most commercially grown varieties. One can usually cut the thorns off as soon as each flower is gathered, so making them far easier to handle.

The florist should ensure that all roses included in gift and presentation bouquets have been adequately conditioned for at least two hours. Roses are one of the most versatile and rewarding of flowers, for we have the promise of the expanding buds day by day. Even when the flower is fully expanded the stem can be cut very short and the bloom floated, which then offers several more days of pleasure. Roses are not particularly suited to the traditional radial design, neither do they really need other flowers with them, though conversely, a few roses with a mixed flower arrangement adds distinction to the design.

Plate 12 shows a tall narrow conical design of mixed roses with a little natural foliage. The container is set on an elegant cut glass platter which adds the necessary visual balance to the design. An all-round arrangement with some lateral emphasis is shown in Plate 13. The colours are grouped so that, although there is a mixture of sizes and colours, the groupings provide visual satisfaction.

One problem with roses is bent neck which means that the rose stem will take up water to within about 3 cm below the bloom only. This results in a limp flower head. Recut the stem end and stand it in really hot water to a depth of about 5 cm. If, after about half an hour, the flower is still not upright, stand the stem end in a little tonic water or other gaseous liquid. If this fails, submerge the flower and the stem, in cool water for several hours. In most instances, this will have the desired effect. However, if the stem is discoloured at the bend, it probably means that the tissues are damaged, and it is doubtful if water will be able to travel past them. If this is the case the only thing to do to save the bloom is to cut the stem here and float the rose.

Sometimes a flower refuses to open, even when others from the same consignment are nicely expanded. This usually indicates that it has been in cool storage for too long or was harvested too early. Try the hot water treatment and place the bud in a good light although unfortunately this does not always work.

Roses are wonderfully varied in shape, form, size and colour. Most of the commercial varieties are blooms on a single stem but more floribunda types are becoming available to the florist and they are very popular. The flowers are smaller and each 'branch' can be divided for use in bridal designs or in arrangements. There are a few in those shown in Plates 12 and 13. Plate 12 shows 'Dorus Rijkers', which has flowers with an almost frilly appearance that make an interesting texture contrast to the larger blooms with creamy petals. The roses to the right of the display basket in Plate 13 are 'Porcelina' which is a charming little rose. Yet another example of a floribunda rose, 'Red Ace', is included in the centre of this design.

Keen gardeners and flower arrangers will know many other types of roses tolerant to the British climate, but which are not grown commercially. For example, the bourbon and damask roses are wonderfully decorative, but are too thorny for cutting or arranging. Another very lovely variety is *Rosa moyesii* 'Geranium' which produces showy deep red single flowers followed by large lantern-shaped hips in late summer.

There are many roses available to the florist nowadays, and the following list is by no means exhaustive.

FLORIBUNDAS	
White	'White Weekend', 'White Dream'
Pink	'Mimi Rose', 'Pink Delight', 'Evelien'
Cream	'Porcelina'
Apricot	'Dorus Rijkers'

Red	'Red Ace'
Mauve	'Joy'

SINGLE VARIETIES	
White	'White Masterpiece' 'Jack Frost', 'Tiara', 'Athena', 'White Success'
Cream	'Champagne', 'Roselandia' (slightly more lemon)
Pink	'Bridal Pink', 'Veronica', 'Pink Success', 'Carole'
Yellow	'Cocktail 80', 'Golden Times', 'Evergold', 'Aalsmeer Gold', 'Diana'
Apricot	'Europa', 'Lorena', 'Lawa', 'Darling', 'Golden Emblem'
Orange	'Belinda', 'Mercedes', 'Sabrina', 'Ilseta'
Red	'Baccara', 'Carambole', 'Allegro', 'Ilona', 'Red Success', 'Madelon', 'Garnet', 'Gabriella', 'Jaguar'
Peach	'Sonia', 'Gerdo'
Two-tone	'La Minuette', 'Candia'

Roses are now available from the florist all year round, even at Christmas. But roses from the garden, in their proper season, will always have a particular appeal. For example, every gardener knows the excitement of cutting the first rose of the year and then, during an unusually mild autumn, the amazement of finding one still in bloom in December. And even with no garden, you can still have a rose bush, for the miniature types have been developed with the windowsill gardener in mind.

11

FLOWERS AS GIFTS

Many special occasions, such as prize-givings and speech days, take place during the summer months. Bouquets given at such times are best composed of mixed flowers. For example, carnations, roses, spray carnations and alstroemeria in mixed tints with a frosting of gypsophila would look lovely.

Unfortunately, because some last longer than others, it has been thought that certain flowers are incompatible with others. In most instances, this is totally incorrect; after all, each individual flower is a separate entity, a commercial bunch of ten apparently identical flowers may not develop evenly and all ten will certainly not expire at the same moment. Even so, when planning mixed bunches and designs, it is still prudent to select flowers that are not too dissimilar in their lasting potential.

PRESENTATION
HAND-TIED BOUQUETS

These are great favourites, both with the public and designers, for almost any effect is possible. In essence, the materials are arranged entirely in the hand, and are finally tied in one place with the stems cut to an even length so that the bouquet can be put into a container without being untied and rearranged.

When this design is demonstrated, it looks really easy to assemble, but, in reality, it is far from simple. It demands considerable muscular control, a true eye and a certain amount of knack which comes with long practice. So do not despair if it does not come right at the first attempt.

The objective is to create a bouquet that shows every flower to advantage. There are numerous designs, the most usual being completely circular with a gently-domed profile. Some materials may be recessed but, in this design, the majority of them are all at the same level with space between each flower. The materials pivot on a central axis within the hand. One of the easiest ways to see how this happens is to take a bundle of wires, holding them in the centre so that the bunch is completely upright (see figure 18). Gently tap the bench with the lower tips of the wires, at the same time slightly releasing your grip in the centre.

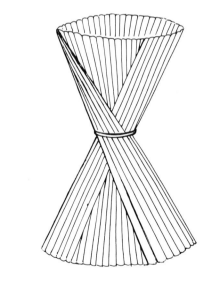

18. *Demonstrating the principle of the hand-tied bouquet using wires*

Assemble the flowers and thoroughly clean every stem. Then lay the materials, including the foliage, in separate groups on the workbench. Also have some little

PLATE 10

*Display pedestal of late spring flowers with eremurus,
delphinium, moluccella, alchemilla, roses and lilies*

PLATE 11

*An all-round design in a simulated wood compote of
mixed flowers including ixia, alstroemeria,
September flower, solidaster, cornflower, alchemilla
and a few 'Harlekijn' spray chrysanthemum*

PLATE 12

*A pyramid centrepiece of mixed roses in a glass
compote set on a crystal base*

PLATE 13

*Roses, grouped in colour and variety to create visual
impact, in a two-handled shallow gift basket*

PLATE 14

Basket with roses, white bouvardia, alchemilla,
September flower and trachelium

PLATE 15

*Parallel form arrangement in a shallow basket with paeony,
trachelium, liatris, sweet William and allium*

PLATE 16

*Campanula, cynara and moluccella for an early
summer arrangement*

PLATE 17

*Geranium flowers and golden cupressus foliage make
a compact and long-lasting centrepiece. Cut
geraniums are sometimes neglected as vase flowers,
but they offer wonderful colour and form variation
as well as interesting foliage.*

bunches of foliage handy to place between some of the flower stems where required. This helps to separate the flowers but must not be inserted between every stem otherwise the tying point will be far too thick and clumsy. It does not matter which hand is used as the 'vase' but, having decided, do not change hands. If you are normally right-handed, you will probably use the left hand to hold the flowers, feeding in from the right (see figure 19).

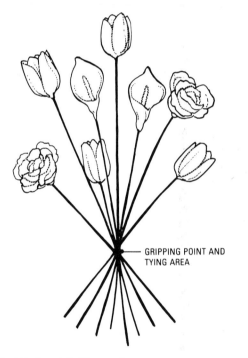

19. *The hand-tied bouquet*

GRIPPING POINT AND TYING AREA

When attempting this for the first time, you may find that the materials refuse to spread out from the 'axis' within your hand, and that you finish up with the usual flat-backed sheaf. In that case try placing one stem in front and the next behind and you will find that this automatically introduces volume to the bouquet. Be quite certain that each stem is laid parallel to the previous one and that the point of contact within your hand is always in the same spot.

The joy of this design is that, should a stem be misplaced, you can immediately extract it and re-position. When all materials have been inserted, bind the stems firmly above your hand. Use raffia, string or plastic tape but never wire as this will cut the stems. Bind around two or three times, pulling firmly and tightly, make a loop and pull the running end through. Then, for extra safety, bring it down between the stems and right up again against the tying area. Cut all stems to the same level.

It is not usual to wrap these bouquets for presentation, but if protection is necessary, roll the design in cellophane, gather the paper together over the flowers and secure with a multi-loop ribbon bow. Tie the cellophane at the axis as well, so that the bouquet can be handled easily.

When attempting a hand-tied bouquet for the first time, it is a good idea to use only one type of flower, such as carnations. They can, of course, be in mixed colours but, since the stems are usually strong and straight and the flowers an even size, it will be easier for you to see the 'bones' of the bouquet. Be sure to put a small cushion of foliage between each stem and add a little September flower, gypsophila, trachelium or *Alchemilla mollis* to introduce another texture.

Any type of flower is suitable for a hand-tied bouquet and the more proficient you become, the more you can experiment with various shapes and sizes. Arum lilies, grasses, heliconia or strelitzia would be outstandingly dramatic, but difficult to control and hold.

CELLOPHANE-WRAPPED BOUQUETS

This is a charming way to gift-wrap flowers for, not only do they look attractive, the cellophane also protects the flowers in transit.

Like anything else created by hand, it takes a little time but this can be minimised if all the necessary items are handy. Choose a multi-loop bow which will either blend in colour or contrast with the flowers and assemble a stapler, a sachet of flower food, the message card and envelope, a care card and the cellophane. It will also be necessary to choose suitable foliage to complement the flowers. If you are in an area where most customers have their own gardens, try to include some that is not generally grown locally for an unusual look. Town dwellers without gardens will obviously appreciate more foliage, but never use cupressus for a gift bouquet as it is not suitable for vase designs.

Before use check that every stem is clean, that the foliage is cut into usable lengths and that it is not too woody. Roses should all be meticulously de-thorned. Next, arrange flowers and foliage to their best advantage. Gladioli can be difficult because of their very long flower heads and so other flowers, when arranged with gladioli, should be placed well up in the bouquet so that the finished effect is not too elongated. Shorter-stemmed flowers, such as freesia and anemones, should be placed nearer the tying point. Place a little light foliage behind them so that they are displayed to look important.

Tie the bow firmly to the bouquet and then lay the bouquet on the cellophane with enough length to cover all the stems up to the tying point. Bring the longer end of the cellophane over the flowers right down to the tying point. Pleat the cellophane just above the bow and secure with one staple. This will ensure that there is enough paper over the flowers so that none is squashed. Keep the bow and tying ends outside the cellophane (see figure 20).

Carefully fold the cellophane towards the bow from each side of the bow. Staple it just once each side to keep it in place. Then take the long tying ends of the ribbon, cross

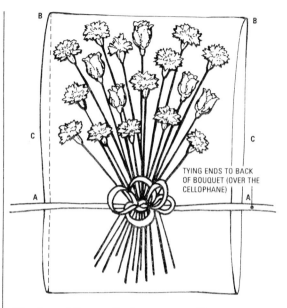

TYING ENDS TO BACK OF BOUQUET (OVER THE CELLOPHANE)

20. *Assembling a cellophane-wrapped bouquet:*
—*Assemble bouquet and tie with ribbon, leaving two very long ends.*
—*Lay bouquet on cellophane so that there is enough paper to fold over both stems and flowers and to meet or slightly overlap at tying point.*
—*Make a pleat in the fold covering flowers at centre. This gives extra 'lift' to the cellophane so that it does not crush the flowers.*
—*Gently fold cellophane at point A towards the tying point and staple once. Then fold tying ends towards back of bouquet, cross them and bring to the front and tie securely through bow.*
—*Fold outer edges of cellophane inwards once at B and C, and staple.*

them behind the bouquet and bring to the front. Tie them firmly, either across the centre of the bow or just above it. If the tying ends are not long enough to do this take another piece of ribbon and tie it around, finishing either across the centre of the bow or just above it. Staple each side of the parcel at the top corners, and once or twice between these and the ribbon bow. Do not seal too firmly or the cellophane will mist over as the flowers respire.

Fix the card's envelope just above the bow so that it can easily be read by the driver.

FLOWERS IN BOXES

These are easily transported by the florist as the boxes can be piled on top of one another in the delivery vehicle.

Line the box with tissue paper, leaving enough outside to fold loosely over the flowers. Position the foliage first and then add the flowers, which can either be arranged at both ends of the box or at one end only. Stems should be carefully placed as parallel to one another as possible, so that the recipient can extract each one easily without damaging the flowers. Give the bouquet a light spray and finish with a ribbon bow.

Secure the lid with Sellotape and add a second bow, if required, at the end of the box, together with the message card.

BASKETS

There is an enormous variety of baskets in many shapes, sizes and textures. They have become one of the most popular of containers for they are suitable for almost any occasion. Technically, a basket should have volume and usually a handle. If the design is intended for presentation, then the flowers should be kept well below the handle, so that it can easily be held in one hand without decapitating the main flowers.

On the other hand, should the basket be for display purposes, then it is acceptable to bring flowers and foliage above the handle, as shown in Plates 14 and 15. But do allow the handle to be seen for, otherwise, there is no point in its being there at all. In the majority of cases, the design should be seen from any angle, though if it is going to be held for any length of time, one side should be less flowery than the other, so that it does not have to be grasped in outstretched hand

to keep it away from the body. Plate 13 shows a shallow oval basket with two very small handles. Even so, these must still be seen, so the design has been angled so that both handles are visible.

Some baskets have a thin plastic lining but I think the basket looks more convincing without it, so this is first removed. Also it is not possible to fix a foam block really firmly on to this lining.

Prepare a plastic container with soaked foam. Obviously, the foam can just be soaked in clear water, but the addition of the merest touch of domestic bleach, about half a teaspoonful to a litre of water, will provide a germ inhibitor which will quite likely help to prolong the vase life of the flowers for at least another day. A nutrient solution, in which the flowers should have been conditioned, not only feeds them but provides a germ inhibitor, both of which contribute to a longer vase life. It therefore seems logical to extend these precautions to the foam in which the flowers will be arranged. If the basket is for presentation, make sure that the foam is totally firm by attaching it to the container with tape. This container can, of course, be fixed to the basket with a glue gun, but then it is not easy to detach. The same applies if Oasis-fix is used, for the fix gets in amongst the weave of the basket and leaves it in a very messy state. So cut a strip of masking tape and fix to the place in the basket where you plan to put the container. The adhesive will then be fixed to the masking tape, which can be peeled off, leaving the basket completely clean. This method is also useful for fixing a container to wood, for example, in a church.

If time permits, leave the basket to settle for some time before making the design, because Oasis-fix adheres more firmly in time, although it never sticks like cement or glue.

Begin inserting masking material as low down into the foam as possible, for the finished design should appear to be originating from the basket and not from the container.

The display basket in Plate 14 is designed on the three-point facing method. The ribbon was attached to the handle, as was the bow, before placing any of the flowers. The roses were then inserted first, to emphasise the strong perpendicular line. This is echoed by one stem of white bouvardia which is also inserted laterally and towards the front of the arrangement. September flower, trachelium and a few stems of *Alchemilla mollis* are finally added.

The basket shown in Plate 13 is also intended for display, rather than for presentation. It would be suitable for placement almost anywhere in the home, or maybe in a shop window—perhaps a bookstore or jeweller's—for a special promotion. Roses, both floribunda and single blooms, are featured, being grouped in colour so that the 'pattern' is evident. The only foliage added is bear grass formed into loops at either end of the design.

The shallow basket in Plate 15 has been used to display a parallel form arrangement —a less traditional design.

DECORATED GIFTS

However modest or however lavish the gift, its value is always enhanced with attractive presentation. Customers sometimes bring their own gifts to the florist to be decorated with flowers and from time to time I have been quite astonished at their trust. For example, a diamond engagement ring to be mounted in an arrangement—I was thankful the gentleman came quite late in the day for the offering to be delivered that evening, because such a bauble was rather too much responsibility in a busy workroom!

Descending to more everyday gifts, a bottle of wine looks wonderful when transformed with a mini-bouquet and some ribbon. Before fixing, tape the neck of the bottle for ribbon will never grip directly to the glass. Tie the ribbon bow to the design, then tie it firmly around the bottle and across another small bow at the back. Attach the decoration at the base of the bottle neck so that the cork can still be drawn without having to detach the flowers.

Just one red rose would look charming tied with silver or gold ribbon, but if time permits, a mixed design made in the hand enhances the gift even more, say, several miniature zinnias, a stem of antirrhinum with a little *Asparagus sprengeri* or foliage from *Geranium* 'Elegante' which is edged with crimson in high summer. This would be in keeping with red wine, but for white wine, choose 'cooler' flower colours; for example, cream alstroemeria and small white roses with loops of chlorophytum foliage.

Of course, summer is not the only season for gifts, far from it, but flowers are more plentiful, certainly in the garden. It is exciting how something quite mundane, say, a plate of biscuits, can be elevated to the special level by the addition of a few short-stemmed flowers—pansies, for example. Providing they have been conditioned first, it is surprising how long they last out of water.

FLOWERS FOR THE
NEW BABY

There are some entrancing designs in cradles, which can be used as a container for a delicate arrangement, or may be filled with flower heads based in foam to resemble the cradle coverlet, with a small corsage added. Val Spicer Designs includes some very appealing examples, including a stork base and a basinette, both of which look charming when dressed with flowers.

But the arrangements must have a light touch. Large, heavy flowers, dark foliage and sombre colours would be totally out of place. This is an occasion when a mixture of small flowers, freesia, tiny roses, lily-of-the-valley, heather, muscari and maybe a touch of September flower would be appropriate.

In France, some arrangements tor the birth of a baby are created in, of course, fresh flowers, but are also imitated with everlastings. Although, unfortunately, the fresh flower design eventually fades, the everlasting prototype can be kept as a memento of this particularly happy occasion.

BOWS

A ribbon finish is essential to almost any gift. Although the flowers themselves look beautiful, the addition of a lavish bow gives tremendous impact to the presentation.

There are many lovely ribbons available, and the final choice must be a personal one. However, the ribbon must be water-resistant, otherwise it may become floppy and diminish rather than enhance the final effect.

Polypropylene ribbon is suitable for most trimmings. It tears easily to decrease its width if required. There are various textures and a multitude of appealing colours. Each reel contains approximately 91 metres. It is by no means expensive but, even so, try to work directly from the reel, rather than cutting off a length at random which may be either too short or too long.

There are several types of bow all of which are attractive. Whichever method is chosen, the bow must be the correct size for the gift. It should never swamp the flowers, either in size or colour, neither should it be so modest as to look mean or apologetic. There are several methods that can be used.

1. Having decided on the size of the loop (i.e. from the centre of the bow to its outer edge) make one loop. Then fold the ribbon over and over to twice the length of the first

loop. Grasp these double loops firmly in the centre, and fold one half precisely on to the other, so that all loops are laying flat together. This acts as a check that all loops are identical in size. Still holding the centre very firmly, cut two neat obliques at each side of the centre (see figure 21).

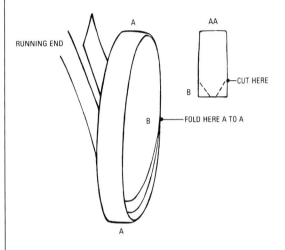

21. *Notching the ribbon to tie a bow*

Next, open out the double loops so that the oblique cuts become notches. Take a narrow piece of the same ribbon and tie across the centre very tightly. The two oblique cuts (now notches) make this possible, for if you try to tie without cuts, the looped ribbon will prove to be too thick, and your anchor ribbon will slip.

Hold the tied centre firmly and pull each loop sideways; one to the right of the centre, the next to the left and so on until all loops have been shaped.

When you try this method for the first time, use half-width ribbon which will not be so difficult to control.

2. Make a loop to the required size, leaving a short trail.

Make another loop of equal size and opposite to the first one, that is, one above and one below the centre. Twist the ribbon at the centre which will help to diminish the bulk. Subsequent pairs of loops should be placed at a slightly different angle so that they do not all lie parallel to one another.

This method needs a very firm hand but, with practice, the bow can be made very quickly. When enough loops are made, tie a thin piece of the same ribbon across the centre, again very tightly. If necessary, adjust the loops to give volume to the bow.

3. Working from the reel, leave an end of ribbon, then make one loop to the required size and fasten it very firmly with several twists of fine silver reel wire. Make sure that this first loop is thoroughly firm, then pull the running end (the one attached to the reel of ribbon) away from the centre fixing, so that no ribbon is left slack underneath (see figure 22).

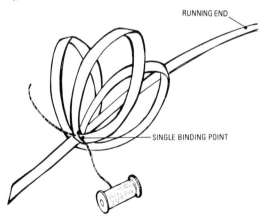

RUNNING END

SINGLE BINDING POINT

22. *Multi-loop bow*

Make a second loop matching the first one in size, and bring the silver wire around this loop attaching it to the first one. This is done with *one* turn of the wire only. Again pull the running end firmly, then make a third loop, each time binding with the silver wire in the same place as before. Make quite sure

that your binding is, in fact, in the same place, otherwise you will find that your bow has several centres instead of one neat one.

Continue to add loops until the bow is large enough. Then wind the silver wire around the binding point so that it holds really firmly. Cut it off close to the ribbon. Cut the running end off to a length similar to the first one. Finally, tie a length of ribbon across the binding point.

Each of these methods takes far longer to describe than to do. All bows should be made with care, as ribbon, however reasonable in price, must not be wasted, for even small off-cuts add up to a significant quantity through a year.

FIGURE OF EIGHT OR BUTTERFLY BOW There are many uses for this simple bow; for example, it is particularly suitable for finishing a sympathy spray, or trimming a basket, a plant or a gift bow.

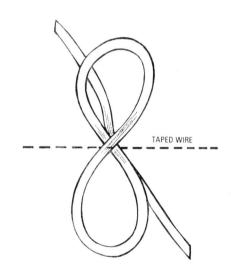

TAPED WIRE

23. *The figure of eight bow*

Tape the centre 5 cm of a 0.56 or 0.70 mm gauge wire. Keeping the ribbon flat, curve it around like a figure of eight, leaving a short length either side (see figure 23). Place the taped wire across the centre and twist firmly twice around itself not around the ribbon. The two wires can then be inserted into the base of the design. If more than two loops are needed, just add several more.

12

SUMMER WEDDINGS

Of course, not all weddings take place in spring and summer, but this is, generally speaking, the most popular time of year. There is an exciting choice of flowers from simple garden varieties to sophisticated orchids, stephanotis, eucharis lilies, lily-of-the-valley and agapanthus.

For arrangements there is a wonderfully wide choice including gladioli, molucella and eremurus as well as the charming campanula in both blue and white. Plate 16 shows a tall ceramic container with campanula plus a few stems of molucella and a little cynara. The flowers are arranged in foam which is supported in the Japanese method: cut the foam almost to fit the neck of the container. Sharpen the point of a thin cane and drive it horizontally through the foam at whatever level is required. That is, if you need about 4 cm of foam above the rim of the container, the cane must be placed so that when it rests on the rim, that amount of foam is above. Also there should be enough foam below the cane to reach the water in the container. The object of the cane is to prevent the foam being driven right down into the vase as stems are inserted.

Normally one would cut each end of the cane off almost level with the rim of the container so that it is not seen. In this case one end has purposely been left at the right of the vase, just under the molucella.

Should it be necessary to add more water to the vase it is possible to take the whole design out and then replace after filling up.

The final choice of flowers will obviously be dictated partly by cost and partly by what is available in long-lasting materials—lilies, liatris, alstroemeria, spray chrysanthemums, anthurium, carnations, gladioli, green amaranthus, achillea—while foliage in summertime fortunately does not pose quite such a problem. Variegated weigela, pieris, large ivy, rhododendron, pittosporum and camellia are just a few useful foliages, while the larger leaves of *Alchemilla mollis* are wonderful for masking the foam.

However, even though the foliage in summer is more mature than earlier in the year, it should still be carefully conditioned, hostas, in particular, needing to be totally immersed for several hours.

One flower that is usually thought of as a pot plant only is geranium. In high summer, the stems are long, the foliage is strong and the flowers are wonderful for quick decoration and colour impact. They are one of the most good-natured of all pot plants, since they tolerate very dry conditions and still reward one with masses of flowers, so generously, in fact, that one can cut from several plants and scarcely leave a gap! Since they are happy in hot sunshine, they would be most useful for marquee use. However, one needs a private supply since the cut flowers are not a commercial product. Plate 17 shows how delightful this flower can look in a long-lasting centrepiece.

Plates 9 and 10 show designs intended for a country wedding in late spring or early summer. The pink theme is carried through from the pedestal arrangement, to the bridal bouquet and pew end illustrated here at the chancel rail, while the auto-corso also contains matching flowers. All were designed in accordance with the bride's chosen colour scheme, relative to the bridal bouquet which includes lilies ('Rosita'), spray roses ('Pink Delight'), a few spray carnations and September flower (Monte Cassino). This is in season for most of the year and introduces a lightness to any design.

The all-white designs (Plates 18 and 19) are for a town ceremony. The bride requested a sheaf which was created with white anthurium, hosta foliage, a little chlorophytum and emphasised with a large satin ribbon. The flowers remained on their natural stems. The head-dress contains stephanotis, September flower and white roses. The display arrangement contains white anthurium, gladiolus, white lilies plus groups of white spray roses ('White Dream') and a matching ribbon.

The design shown in Plate 20 was intended as a table centrepiece for a pearl wedding, but would be equally suitable for a wedding reception. Designed in parallel form, and based on a large white oval dish, it contains white roses, bouvardia and allium. This design would also be appropriate if white candles were exchanged for the central column of flowers.

the all-round vase design, the five units should be the same length, but each set of units must be a different length so that, in profile, the posy describes a gentle curve towards and away from the central flower.

Following the basic recipe, it will be seen that 43 flowers and buds are needed, plus 28 leaves, preferably in varying sizes. A bud or a smaller leaf should be placed at the tip of each unit with the larger material added which will be towards the centre of the design. Keep the flower units and the foliage units entirely separate. If you mix flowers and foliage on one unit, the finished effect may be somewhat confused.

But to be more specific, let us imagine a simple hand posy of pink spray carnations and the pink roses such as 'Mimi Rose', or 'Carol'. For foliage we will use *Hedera* 'Glacier' plus some green rose hips, probably the lantern-shaped ones from *Rosa moyesii* 'Geranium'. These, of course, turn a rich scarlet in late summer so would not be

A Five-point Posy—Basic Minimum Recipe

Roses			Spray Carnations			Foliage		
Units	Flowers	Total	Units	Flowers	Total	Units	Leaves	Total
5 ×	2	= 10	5 ×	2	= 10	5 ×	3	= 15
8 ×	1	= 8	5 ×	1	= 5	5 ×	2	= 10
						3 ×	1	= 3
		18			15			28

The figures on the left indicate how many units. The figures on the right denote how many single flowers, buds or leaves are on each unit. This recipe can only be a guideline because, obviously, the number of flowers on each unit must be dictated by the size of each flower or floret. For example, if you are working with stephanotis you would require more flowers than if you had chosen spray chrysanthemum. The same concept applies to the foliage units. However, at least two layers of units of both flowers and foliage are required. Exactly like

appropriate to this design unless they are still green.

Collect the ivy leaves in varying sizes. Wire each one and grade them, so that for the first five units there is a fairly small one for the tip, a medium leaf for the next one down and a slightly larger one for leaf number three. Leave a larger space between the first and second leaves, but place the third one closer. This will give an impression of flow and movement. The leaves should be wired on 0.32 mm silver wire and mounted on to a 0.70 mm 'backbone'. When this is completed, put each unit into a bowl of clean water. This will help to keep all materials fresh until you are ready to assemble them.

Build five more units, wired and mounted on similar size wires, but these only need two leaves on each.

Choose three larger leaves, wire them on 0.32 mm wire and mount on 0.56 mm wire. These are to place deep down in the posy much in the same way as one puts larger foliage towards the centre of a vase arrangement.

The rose hips should be wired on either 0.56 or 0.70 mm gauge according to how 'woody' they feel. Wire at least five singly plus three more, also singly if the design seems to need them.

The spray carnations and buds will be wired on 0.56 mm gauge then mounted on 0.70 mm wire into units.

One set of rose units will consist of a bud and one partly open flower (5 × 2). These are also mounted on 0.70 mm wire as all roses are relatively heavy. Wire eight single blooms on 0.56 mm or 0.70 mm, five to be inserted as another flower layer and three to form the centre line. These, also, should be put in singly so that you have total control over their placement.

First take the centre flower and measure a lateral against it, in order to decide where the tying point shall be. Twice the length of the first lateral units will determine the spread of the posy and as the profile is to be domed and not conical, the centre flower is usually placed slightly below the edge flower of the first lateral. Having decided on the position of your tying point add the other four laterals in parallel with the first one around the centre flower unit. Bind firmly at the centre point (the lower down the unit this is, the larger will be your posy). Bind to the end of the wires as this will prevent the wires from swivelling on the centre axis.

Then bend the five laterals crisply down at right angles to the centre unit. Make sure that none of them is inclined to move; they must be absolutely firm otherwise the circular outline of the posy will be lost.

Add another set of units, inserting them parallel with the centre unit. Bind again firmly and then bend them at the binding point. Continue to add inserts, but remember that the posy must not be too tightly packed; there should be space between each flower. Finally insert the three larger leaves at the tying point to add visual strength to the design. Insert ribbons, if needed. Cut the handle wires to the required length. The average length is about 14 cm, but a very young child sometimes likes to hold the posy with both hands, so make sure it is long enough.

Add ribbon trails at this stage, if they are required. Remember to tape the wire that secures the ribbon as this helps the wire to bite on to the ribbon. It also presents a better finish.

Bind the handle with tape and finish with ribbon.

AUTUMN

13

FLOWERS FOR AUTUMN DESIGNS

Towards autumn, the days get rapidly shorter, the lawns are not growing so quickly, there is a hint of early frost and we yearn for colour, presumably to compensate for the lack of strong sunlight. Dahlias are frequently advertised as offering bright jewel-like colours, and so they do. Although, broadly speaking, the essence of good flower design is the presence of a certain amount of variation, particularly in flower shapes, there is a wealth of colour variation, size and personality in dahlias. There are the tiny pompon types, solid with petals and just perfect for a boutonniere, the spiky-petalled cactus varieties, the waterlily types and the large opulent-looking decorative ones. They vary in size and some are small enough for a lapel spray or a head-dress, while the larger ones contribute emphasis and strong colour to arrangements. An added bonus is that they are very modest in price. Unfortunately, though, dahlias are easily damaged when bunched and packed for transport to wholesale markets. Some growers do harvest the flowers at precisely the right moment, just before the flower reaches maturity and they also pack them very carefully.

They should be carefully unpacked, the lower foliage stripped off and the stem-end cut with a clean sloping cut. Condition as usual in lukewarm nutrient solution. Their vase life should be at least four days, possibly longer. Dahlias are all tolerant of being arranged in flower foam, though would probably last even longer if only mesh, or a narrow-necked container is used, so that the stems can be directly in the water.

The stems are hollow and it is possible to wire them internally with the hook method, for the small hook will bed right down into the flower should a little control be required as in, for example, bridal work.

Chrysanthemums used to be a traditional autumn flower, but spray varieties are now available all the year round. They are therefore known in the floristry profession as AYR. With so many from which to choose they have, to a certain extent, taken the place of the larger blooms, which are not generally seen in the shops until late August. Even then, it seems far too early, for they are, in my view, more suitable for the weeks around Christmas-time. They are certainly very lovely for large decorations and for special church arrangements, as shown in Plate 23. They have an incredibly long vase life, though the foliage usually withers long before the flower collapses.

We should not overlook the humble nasturtium which sometimes appears uninvited into the garden and seems then to flourish even more ebulliently than when planted in a particular spot! Providing we have no frost, the later flowers usually have good long stems and are ideal for a quick table centrepiece. They prefer to be placed directly in water and not into foam, so choose a slender container and you have a brightly-glowing arrangement in minutes.

In recent years, varieties of Michaelmas Daisy have greatly improved, both in shape, form and colour. The original pastel mauve, which was most unattractive on a grey autumn day, has been superseded by various mauve/red/pink larger flowers, which are ideal for cutting. There are also some very attractive dwarf types, which could even be grown in window boxes and are still useful for cutting for smaller arrangements.

Other colourful flowers we can use at this time of the year include gerbera, zinnia, gladioli, amaranthus (love-lies-bleeding), mid-century hybrid lilies, bouvardia and antirrhinum. All have gorgeous warm glowing colours which are guaranteed to induce cheerfulness into a grey autumn or winter day.

THE USE OF FOLIAGE AND BERRIES

At this time of year we can augment our arrangements by looking out for autumn foliage and fruits. These introduce a variation of texture and colour which can be quite exhilarating. There is no need to emphasise the effect of shiny scarlet holly berries with dark green or variegated foliage. Chinese lantern (*Physalis franchetii*) produces relatively insignificant white flowers with an inflated calyx which, towards autumn, turns from clear green to bright orange—hence the name. These 'lanterns' are very decorative and can be gently opened to reveal a scarlet berry within.

Gardeners can plan to have shrubs and foliage plants of interest for most of the year. *Rosa moyesii* 'Geranium' has already been mentioned but the rich display of colour in the autumn is worth emphasising. The clusters of lantern-shaped hips are not only bright in the garden but they are useful to add to autumn and winter foliage designs.

The spindle tree (*Euonymus europaeus*) is another attractive berry-bearing shrub which produces salmon-pink and orange clusters of small fruits, which, incidentally, are thought to be extremely poisonous. In autumn the foliage turns from fresh green to bronze and red. If branches can be cut just before the fruits split open, they will last indoors for several weeks. The eighteenth-century diarist John Evelyn writes, that the name spindle tree derives from the fact that the wood was used for violin bows, inlay, virginal keys and—slightly more mundane—toothpicks and butchers' skewers. Presumably it was also manufactured into spindles, which were relatively big business at the time of the Industrial Revolution.

14

IMPORTED EXOTICS

When the abundance of native flowers decreases we can turn to imported flowers, many coming from the other side of the world where spring is beginning.

These exotic flowers can be used sparingly as only a few stems will make great impact. When planning to use them, order at least a week in advance so that the wholesaler has time to locate and import them and secondly, to give yourself ample time to condition them thoroughly. Bear in mind that most of the so-called exotics originate in hot climates so condition them in warm nutrient solution and store them at a temperature of at least 12°C completely free of any draught.

However, the success of a design is by no means entirely due to the inclusion of 'exotic' material, but rather to how it is used. For not every design demands expensive material flown in out of season from the other side of the world. Flowers, like people, have personalities. These must be relevant to the design, which in turn should be relevant to the occasion and to the environment.

Anigozanthos, kangaroo paw, is now being imported into Britain. It is not a large family of species but we get at least three varieties here and each adds a particular richness to any display design. They are native to SW Australia so their seasonal availability in Britain is in winter-time. The flowers, which may be green tinged with red, or deep red, really do look like little paws.

Anthurium is a native of Colombia but is also grown in other suitable environments, such as on Hilo, one of the Hawaiian group. Fields of them are grown for export and they look exotic and impressive in white, pink and scarlet. The clear-cut outline of each flower and its shiny surface lift it, without doubt, into the dominant group. The flower is carried on a long smooth stem which is relatively slender. It is ideal for arrangements while the smaller varieties can be used for bridal bouquets, as shown in Plate 18. The so-called 'flower' is a colourful spathe, while the true flower is the rather insignificant spadix in the centre.

Bouvardia is now available almost all year round. Even so, it is still a very special flower and righly deserves a place among the exotics. In white, pink or bright red it can be used in lapel sprays and bouquets as well as decorative arrangements (see Plate 20).

Euphorbia fulgens came originally from Mexico and is also available during our winter season. The colours range from creamy-white through yellow to orange and bright scarlet. It is wonderful for natural bouquets and also for container designs. Providing it is properly conditioned it should have a vase life of at least five days.

Gardenia belongs to the same family as bouvardia (Rubiaceae) and is certainly one of the more special exotics. They make really magnificent pot plants and one plant alone will perfume a whole hothouse. Although we do not see the cut flowers now so frequently, the plants are available already in bud. They require a steady temperature of about 20°C as well as a daily spray with clear water to prevent buds from falling. In spite of their being so apparently tender, they are a delight to grow and to be able to cut a bloom for use as a boutonniere or lapel spray is decidedly rewarding.

The orchid is still probably considered to be the most exotic of all flowers. It belongs to a truly gigantic family, the second largest in the whole vegetable kingdom, containing no less than 18,000 species. In their natural habitat, orchids are surprisingly adaptable, some growing in what could be considered thoroughly inhospitable situations.

There is an aura of romance surrounding them, for people have risked their lives collecting new species; large sums of money are expended on their cultivation while the sheer variety in those thousands of species is breathtaking.

The Flower Council of Holland issues a flower catalogue of commercially grown flowers listing no less than 45 different types of cymbidium orchid: of course, not all are available at the same time and few, if any, during our summer months. Possibly this is one factor that makes them seem so special, for orchids are synonymous with the idea of a hot steamy jungle.

The larger cymbidiums are wonderfully durable and are excellent for a special lapel spray or for inclusion in a bridal bouquet. The smaller types, known as mini-cymbidiums, are about half the size of the others and are ideal, not only for bridal work, but also for special flower arrangements.

Singapore orchids are also very lovely, though in recent years they seem largely to have lost their exotic appeal as they can be seen on sale in every supermarket. But why not? Surely everyone has a right to something special along with the weekly grocery list. These lovely little flowers, mauve, white and some a greeny-yellow with brown stripes, look exotic in a slender vase anywhere in the house. Moreover, they have excellent lasting qualities.

Oncidium orchids are enchanting, very delicate-looking flowers growing in profusion on slender stems. They belong to a group of over 500 types, but this tiny dainty yellow flower is the one most generally seen commercially. For buying, they can be grouped with the ones known as Singapore orchids, but if this particular variety is wanted, then they should be asked for by name. Unlike some of the Singapore orchids, which can be used either individually or on the stem, this particular variety is far too delicate to handle and should be left on the stem. It is delightful for vase designs, or two or three flowers can be cut in a group (still on the main stem) for inclusion in a lapel spray or bouquet, or in a bowl arrangement (see Plate 3).

Protea is the national flower of South Africa being cultivated for export mainly in Cape Province. It is also grown in Hawaii and Madeira. Some varieties have heavy flowers on thick woody stems; needing a great deal of water they last longer if arranged in mesh rather than in foam. They are, in the main, very long-lasting and, if dried, make attractive everlasting designs. One of the most popular for bridal designs is the tiny pink one with papery-like petals called 'Blushing Bride'. These flowers have the appearance of being extremely delicate yet they, too, are woody and are quite difficult to wire.

Protea are so varied in size, shape and colouring that they rarely need other flowers or foliage to complete the design. Foliage from the silver leaf tree (*Leucadendron argenteum*) usually seems the most appropriate, if any is needed. As the name implies, the leaves, which overlap each other all around the stem, completely hiding it, are silver one side and pale grey on the reverse. They, too, are very long-lasting and dry naturally to perfection. Silver leaf foliage is sometimes included in special foliage bunches known as Safari Packs, but if a large quantity is required, it would be advisable to order it separately in advance.

Spathiphyllum is similar to *anthurium*, though not so impressive; it has greenish-white spathes but a more significant 'flower'. This is also used for bridal bouquets, though mostly they are grown as pot plants. They are exceedingly elegant and

PLATE 18

*For a city wedding—an elegant hand-tied sheaf of white
anthurium on natural stems with hosta and chlorophytum
foliage, tied with a lavish bow of white ribbon*

PLATE 19

*A church design in a green and white theme (see also
Plate 18) includes gladioli,* Lilium *'Sterling Star',
roses and anthurium*

PLATE 20

A centrepiece design for a pearl wedding party.
Based on a large white oval dish, allium and white
bouvardia describe the tall central line. White roses
in two shorter parallel lines are placed either side,
while more roses on shorter stems form a terraced
base with white bouvardia.

PLATE 21

*A facing design in a two-handled pottery pitcher
with a strong central line of mauve carnations. Pale
mauve and clove spray carnations form the outline
with* Eucalyptus populus *foliage.*

PLATE 22

Carnations, yellow freesia and spray carnations
compose a modest design suited to almost any season

PLATE 23

*Pedestal arrangement in a deep bowl, with spray
chrysanthemum, long stems of oncidium orchids
highlighted with copper beech foliage*

PLATE 24

An asymmetrical arrangement in an onyx urn
composed of alstroemeria, orchids, carnations and
spray carnations, with cotoneaster foliage to
introduce visual strength

PLATE 25

*A wintertime sympathy wreath edged with ribbon and
laurel foliage. The base of laurel 'cones' is decorated
with a modest top-spray of five yellow roses, holly
foliage and a few stems of variegated euonymus*

contribute emphatically to variation in texture if included in a mixed planting.

Strelitzia, known as the Bird of Paradise, is well known to most flower enthusiasts for it really does resemble a stately bird. The green 'beak', which is, in reality, the flower sheath, expands to release blue and deep yellow bracts which stand up like a cockscomb. These bracts do not emerge all at once, so that the strelitzia is both robust and long-lasting; the perfect flower for arrangements in a warm atmosphere. The stem is very strong, and rather thick, usually measuring about 2 cm in diameter. The foliage also is stiff, each leaf being at least 25 cm long, the perfect complement to the flowers. Strelitzias are also native to South Africa though they will grow wherever there is a moist warm atmosphere with a night temperature of not less than 10°C.

They can, of course, be grown under glass in Britain.

Each flower head is carefully protected with waxed paper for delivery to the market. They are usually sold wholesale in counts of five flowers, which sometimes includes one or two leaves as well. They cost several pounds each, but are well worth it in terms of exciting impact.

These are by no means the only unusual or special flowers we see from time to time. For example, Eucharis lilies are wonderful for a sophisticated bridal bouquet, the greenish centre surrounded by chalk-white petals needing little to complement them.

Datura will also flower when grown in a large container, but it needs a very sheltered position. Pink, red or white, this is a most unusual flower for a special bridal bouquet or used to create impact in a container design.

15

SPECIAL OCCASIONS IN AUTUMN

AUTUMN WEDDINGS

There is something special about a wedding near the traditional harvest time. With reasonable luck, the weather is bright and there are plenty of flowers available. Though some brides prefer to wear clear white, many favour the warmer tints, cream, champagne and even palest amber. These are perfect for early autumn; an all-foliage bouquet with wheat-ears would be lovely for a country wedding.

However, foliage should be very carefully conditioned. If in doubt as to its lasting qualities, be sure to put some on test before including it in the design. That is, condition the leaves as required, either in flower food solution for several hours, or by submerging the whole leaf in cold water. Then wire and tape it and leave it for at least twelve hours. If it is still fresh, then you know that this type of leaf can be included in the bridal design. Unfortunately, some of the most attractive foliage is not reliable for lasting; for example, Virginia creeper foliage turns a vibrant scarlet in late September, but would not last long enough for inclusion in a bridal design.

It is better to rely on a mixture of foliage from some of the hardy garden shrubs with a few leaves from indoor plants, many of which last really well. For colour, the smaller foliage from a mature croton is wonderful. To ensure lasting, after submerging the leaves in water, wire through the central rib with .38 silver wire, then add a tiny piece of damp Kleenex or cotton wool to the stem end before mounting it on .56 or .70, according to its position in the design.

The addition of berries helps to give the bouquet dimension, but do be quite sure that the ones chosen are neither poisonous nor squashy; either could be disastrous! Rose hips are perfectly safe; those from the old-fashioned species roses are very suitable and are also really decorative.

A white and green wedding in autumn is also very lovely. A bouquet of white roses, small white lilies (Sterling Star is a neat shape) *bouvardia* and sprays of white *Euphorbia fulgens* would combine to make a rich and elegant design. Defoliate the *Euphorbia* so that the flowers show to full advantage. And a stem or two of *Symphoricarpos*, also defoliated, but it would be prudent to tuck this deep into the design so that there is no risk of the white berries detaching from the stem. Clear green foliage, for example *Scindapsus aureus* or *Dracaena sanderiana* (green with a white edge) would complement an all-white design and both can be judiciously pruned from house plants. And although *molucella* is a flower it could be used to great effect in place of foliage, either using small sections of the flower head, or by wiring each bell and assembling them into graceful units.

For contrast in an all-white bouquet, gentian would add a touch of drama. These little beauties are available in September and sometimes as early as late August, but if bought through a wholesale market, one needs to make enquiries several weeks beforehand. They are such a piercing blue that one small bunch would achieve the effect.

For the bridesmaids, natural-looking hand-tied bouquets of mixed freesia, a few stems of late lavender with grey lavender foliage would look both appealing and unusual. The addition of a little green or mauve hydrangea in the centre of the designs would underline the colour theme.

The technique of the hand-tied bouquet is described on pp 52–3. Success is not just a question of composing a bunch freestyle; this is an acquired skill for not only must each stem be correctly placed, but the design must be tied firmly in one place so that every flower remains in position.

HALLOWEEN

This age-old festival (31 October) is the occasion for fancy dress parties and for the younger set to visit houses in search of goodies (trick or treat)—a mild version of 'your money or your life'! It is also a wonderful opportunity for the florist to put on special window displays, particularly with dried materials. The witches' brooms and pumpkins will most likely form the basis of the scene, with dried grasses, bouquets of dried flowers and informal baskets. Nothing should be too formal or stylised otherwise the atmosphere will be lost.

Some intriguing materials are to be found in the hedgerows; for example, the giant hogweed, now dried to a lovely pale coffee tint, some of the flowers skeletonised so that the tall stem appears to be supporting numbers of miniature skeleton sunshades. It is worth hunting for one or two of these stems, usually around 2 m tall. They would have to be either supported with a clamp or driven into a large block of dry foam. This base can be masked with natural wood or cork bark and/or a collection of ornamental gourds. These are very easy to grow, though they take up quite a lot of garden space for a few months until the gourds are ready for cutting. But, apart from planting the seeds and transplanting them as seed-

ling stage, they require no special care. Harvest them, if possible, during a dry spell of weather. Paint with a coat of thin varnish and they should last all winter long. (A basket of colourful gourds in the home is also very attractive and makes quite a talking point.)

Wild clematis (Old Man's Beard) is also readily available in many areas; even if you are a city dweller, you probably will not have to drive very far before you find some. Hops also grow wild in some hedgrows, but be sure not to take them from the cultivated hop gardens. They are both aromatic and very decorative and would add personality to your display.

Some colour is needed to add drama to the scene, even though there is the orange pumpkin and the colourful gourds. A line design with several large scarlet anthurium would be very eye-catching. If this seems too formal, an arrangement of scarlet-tinted dried materials would also be appropriate; lotus pods, palm spears, bell cups, loofah pod and seagrape foliage would provide plenty of shapes and texture contrast.

Suggestions for Halloween do not, of course, only apply to florists' window displays. A small pumpkin table centrepiece would be decidedly different from the usual fresh flower arrangement.

GUY FAWKES' NIGHT

Guy Fawkes, or Bonfire Night (5 November) is an opportunity for colourful window display and fun arrangements for the home.

For floral displays in the appropriate explosive spirit, large protea would be ideal; some varieties even resemble a catherine wheel—*Leucospermum catherinae* is, in fact, named for its amazing resemblance to this particular firework. The lily 'Firecracker' would look both exciting and opulent with the leucospermum, while scarlet gerbera and *Euphorbia fulgens* 'Red Surprise' would complete a truly fiery design. These are all very special and the home flower arranger might not feel inclined to make such lavish arrangement. But scarlet spray carnations with larger scarlet carnations and a few stems of copper beech foliage would combine to make an equally eye-catching design on a more modest scale.

REMEMBRANCE SUNDAY

All Saints' Day (1 November) is a very busy occasion for all continental florists, but is not yet observed to the same extent in Britain. It is a special time of remembrance for all departed relatives, and tributes of flowering plants and wreaths are placed on the graves. From the florists' point of view, it is one of the most highly pressurised days in the calendar.

In Britain we observe Remembrance Sunday—the Sunday nearest to 11 November (the date of signing the Armistice ending World War I). Emblems with the traditional remembrance Flanders poppies are laid on memorials. Most of these tributes are based with laurel. If a mossed base is used, then the laurel can be neatly bound on, layer upon layer, but the more usual method in this country is known as 'pinning'.

If the base is mossed the underside should be masked by neatly binding on cupressus. This must be done before the laurel is pinned on.

The neatest finish—and the quickest—is achieved with a Naylorbase frame, since the dark green plastic base ensures that the tribute is clean to handle. First trim the foam edge down carefully so that it is not standing up straight from the plastic edge. This should be done before the base is soaked. Smooth the edge with the flat of your hand so that the profile of the base is gently domed.

Only select leaves with perfect tips. If the rest of the leaf is damaged, this does not matter because most of it (except the top

2 cm) will be hidden underneath another layer of leaves. Grade the leaves, placing about four of similar size together, laying the tips exactly one on top of the other. Then cut right across the lower section of the little bunch. This is done because when they are pinned one on top of the other, the stem area would become bulky and render the final surface uneven (see figure 24).

Cut 0.70 mm wires into short lengths of about 3 cm and bend them into small hairpins. Each leaf should be pinned on separately to ensure that it does not shift. The pin should be positioned approximately 2 cm up from the cut base of each leaf, sufficiently high up so that the tip remains in place, yet not so high as to show when the next leaf is pinned on (see figure 25). For a wreath, work from the outside edge to the centre and back again, to and fro, keeping the tips of the leaves in as straight a line as possible across the ring. You will probably need to use slightly larger leaves for the outer edge and also insert two extra every few rows, to compensate for the larger curve.

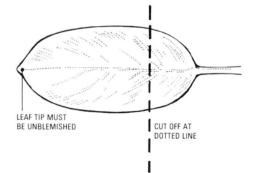

LEAF TIP MUST
BE UNBLEMISHED

CUT OFF AT
DOTTED LINE

24. *Preparation of laurel leaves for a remembrance day tribute*

Having pinned one row, from outer to inner edge, place the next row with the tips precisely in the dip formed by the junction of two leaves in the previous row (see figure 25). The size of tribute will dictate how

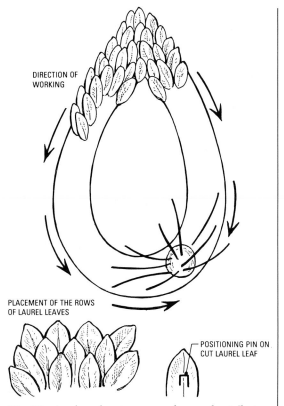

DIRECTION OF WORKING

PLACEMENT OF THE ROWS OF LAUREL LEAVES

POSITIONING PIN ON CUT LAUREL LEAF

25. *Pinning laurel on to a remembrance day tribute*

Never economise with laurel, for it is usually plentiful and, fortunately, not very expensive. However, only use the mature leathery foliage, for new growth will barely last an hour or so. Continue right around the wreath so that the final row of foliage can be tucked under the first row. A top spray of Flanders poppies and foliage can be attached at this point. However, if fresh flowers are used, it may be necessary to fix a foam bun or 'le Bump' to provide extra depth to hold the stems (see p. 78).

A memorial cross will be prepared in the same way, working from the tip of each arm towards the centre.

With a chaplet place the first leaf centrally right at the top. Then pin one row of leaves to the left and right alternately, until the top of the chaplet is covered. The inside row of leaves should point slightly inwards so that the tips meet. Decide on the position of the top spray and work down each side, one side at a time, towards this area. Fix the top spray in the same way as described for the wreath. When all the foliage is in place, clean it gently with a damp paper tissue and clean water, then spray lightly with leaf-shine. Laurel-based tributes with a top spray of holly, suitable foliage and berries are also in demand at Christmas-time for placing on a family grave.

many leaves need to be placed on each row; an average size would probably need about five leaves one way and four the other.

16

SYMPATHY DESIGNS

The impact of flowers at a funeral can have quite unexpected and sometimes far-reaching repercussions. The majority of people attending are usually in an extremely vulnerable state of mind. There are those who are so grief-stricken that they are unable to register any of the designs. On the other hand there are others who enjoy looking at the tributes and who derive a certain amount of solace from the flowers. People are quick to appreciate an appealing design but are, understandably, equally quick to condemn a poor one.

So it is absolutely vital that no effort is spared for every single design that we send to a funeral, no matter how modest, to look fresh and crisp. Moreover, it is as well to bear in mind that, even if the immediate family is not able to inspect each tribute objectively at the time of the funeral, it is quite likely that some of them will return the next day to have another look. Cards must be clearly written or typed when not inscribed by the client. Each card should be covered with a cellophane envelope or piece of clear film as protection from the weather. Finally, the card must be fixed on the tribute in a prominent position so that everyone can easily read the inscription.

BASES

Traditionally these are of wire and they come in various sizes, particularly the wreath and cross frames. If a special design is required, it can usually be made by the wireworker within a few days.

The cushion, pillow, open book and heart frames are constructed in two parts; a flat base and a slightly raised top. Moss is inserted between these and the two sides are then wired closely together.

The foam, which has to be soaked, as for a flower arrangement, is stabilised on either a polystyrene or a firm plastic base, according to the manufacturer. The Naylorbase products include all the main shapes in varying sizes, plus letters, numbers and other specific designs which are illustrated in their colour brochure. All are made in foam which is laminated to a high-quality plastic base.

The polystyrene bases are produced by Millfield Florist Sundries, the larger sizes being reinforced for extra strength. The foam used is a Bloomfix product which is very reliable, and the brown polystyrene base will tolerate woody stems and wired material being inserted. Thus, the total depth of foam can be used for the flowers. Before soaking it, spray the brown edge with dark green Oasis-spray which greatly improves the appearance.

It must be a matter of personal preference whether wire frames or the manufactured bases are used, depending on what suits you best. It is also advisable to confer with your local funeral directors because some of them dislike the manufactured bases because, they say, the flowers fall out. However, this indicates that the florist is not using the base properly, rather than being a fault of the base itself.

Yet, on the other side of the coin, some funeral directors dislike tributes on mossed bases and will not accept them if it can possibly be avoided. Quite likely this is because they have had to handle heavy, dripping designs from time to time.

To moss a wreath or cross, first soak the moss since wires will not drive easily into dry moss. Soaking the base once the moss has been applied is not very successful, because it may result in the wrong tension in some places. Moss which is bought from the wholesale market is usually supplied rolled into little bundles. Tease it out so that it is light and manageable. If it is too damp, squeeze out the excess moisture. Using bobbin wire or string, bind small handfuls to the frame as evenly as possible. Do not over-moss, for this will produce a very stodgy result. It is always possible to add more moss, but not as easy to extract it once it has been wired in place. Each bind should be about 2 cm apart and the tension will be governed by how much moss is applied and how tightly the binding wire is pulled (see figure 26). Work from right to left, if you are right-handed: from the left if you are left-handed.

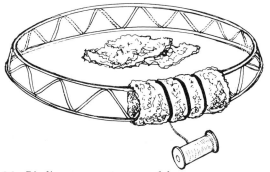

26. *Binding moss on to a wreath base*

For a cross, begin at one end and work towards the centre. Then go to the other end and do likewise. Then to the end of each arm, finishing in the centre. Moss the ends as squarely and firmly as possible.

The underside (back) of the tribute should always be neatened. This can be done by binding small pieces of evergreen on or by attaching large ivy leaves or laurel foliage, either by binding or by pinning each leaf with a hairpin cut from 0.56 or 0.70 mm wire. This does not take so long as it sounds and, with practice, can be a quick operation.

Edging

Not all designs require an edging, the main purpose of which is to protect the flowers in handling and to provide an attractive finish. The fashion now is to edge with ribbon, which is very attractive, but which is not appropriate to every tribute. There are a number of foliages suitable for edging, provided they have good lasting properties. Cupressus, laurel and camellia are all reliable though cupressus is more generally used.

Cut the cupressus into pieces about 6 cm long. Gather several pieces into one hand; hold tightly to one end with your finger and thumb while fanning the other end out as much as possible. Using 0.90 or 0.70 mm wire, 12–14 cm long, make a loop with the top 3 cm of wire. Lay it under your thumb on the base of the foliage fan, bind the longer end of wire around the shorter end and the foliage twice (see figure 27). This is very repetitive time-consuming work, but the edging can be prepared in any quiet moments in the shop. It will last a week or

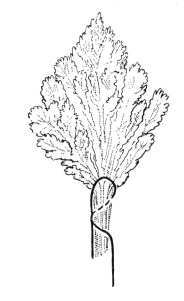

27. *Cupressus edging for a sympathy design*

more if neatly stacked in a small box and stored in a cool, dark place.

Camellia edging can be made by selecting leaves of a similar size. Wire them, using the loop method, with 0.70 or 0.90 mm wire. Do not use the stitch method as it may mark the foliage and spoil the appearance of the edging. Laurel foliage should be cleaned and graded. Then take three leaves of similar size and gently fold them inwards. Take care not to make a crease or crack along the centre of the leaves. Drive a 0.90 mm wire through the base of these three leaves so that they are secured at the base and fan out at the tips. Pinch the two pieces of wire together at the spot where they have pierced the leaves. If this does not hold them steadily, wind one end of wire around the other, similar to the cupressus technique.

Any ribbon used for edging must be water-resistant. The ribbon is folded to a depth of about 2 cm, and a similar fold is made so that the two folds meet (see figure 28). The whole pleat will then measure 4 cm across. Do not crease the ribbon, but simply staple each fold once as you make it. Continue this process, making sure that every fold is the same width. Work directly from the bolt of ribbon so as to be certain that you have enough ribbon and that none is wasted. However, as a rough guide, the amount of ribbon needed is at least three times the overall edge-length of the tribute, a fact that will help in calculating the cost of the edging.

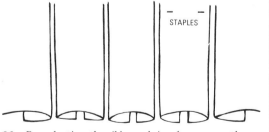

28. *Box pleating the ribbon edging for a sympathy design*

When edging a cushion or pillow with ribbon there are four corners to contend with. As you get near to the corner, make the pleat a little smaller. It will take about five pleats to 'turn' the corner. If the same size pleat is used all the way around the edge, a somewhat stretched appearance will be obtained at the corners. Polypropylene ribbons are not expensive so one can use them generously.

Ribbon edging is most easily attached to a mossed base with ordinary steel pins which are bought from the wholesaler. Drive each pin through the ribbon pleat at the top and into the moss diagonally. Use the same method for the manufactured bases on polystyrene but use a glue gun for those with plastic bases.

CHOICE OF TRIBUTE

Tributes can be either formal or informal. The formal group includes wreath, cross, heart, pillow, cushion and other special designs such as an open book, vacant chair or Gates of Heaven.

When is a formal design appropriate? As most of these are traditional tributes, they are always suitable. Some people feel that they have a somewhat stiff appearance, though they are frequently chosen as family tributes. However, some clients have a completely open mind about what they would like so the florist should be able to advise if necessary. This is where a design catalogue is a great help. It may not be feasible to reproduce the exact flower content, because of cost or seasonal variation, but at least it gives the client an insight into what type of designs can be produced.

The James Naylor Organisation has produced a design book in full colour which is. both helpful and very attractive. The two British relay organisations, British Tele-flower and Interflora, also have their own catalogues, which indicate to a prospective client the types of designs that can be supplied in another part of the country. However, as with bridal designs, anyone can photograph his or her own work and compile a catalogue of known and tried designs. If these are produced in duplicate, one set might be given to the local funeral director who can also use it as a guide to availability. At these stressful times, people are averse to having to make too many visits and, since they usually contact the funeral director first, it seems logical that he should take orders as your agent, assuming that he is happy with your work.

For funerals in autumn and winter it is sometimes difficult to produce a tribute which is sufficiently impressive for the occasion. But they need not be made all in flowers, for some foliage is at its best. The design in Plate 25 shows a medium-sized wreath based in laurel foliage, with a top spray of only five roses with sprays of euonymus foliage. This is a wonderfully versatile shrub, though somewhat slow-growing, so should only be cut sparingly.

The texture of the base is varied by making little cones of laurel foliage, first cleaning and grading the leaves. Taking them one at a time, cut close to the central vein upwards from the base of the leaf to about 3 cm. Then cut at right angles right across the central vein to the edge of the leaf (see figure 29). You will then have a leaf with one long and one short lobe. Roll the leaf around your forefinger so that the longer piece is on the outside. Still keeping your finger inside the cone, drive a 0.70 mm wire through the base of the cone, removing your finger at the last moment.

An example of a simple understated summertime wreath is shown in Plate 26. The ring is based with reindeer moss pinned on with small hairpins cut from 0.70 mm wire. The moss should be well soaked before use as it is usually stiff and dry when first bought. The three groups of flowers arranged in semi-parallel form include liatris, sweet William, alstroemeria and green

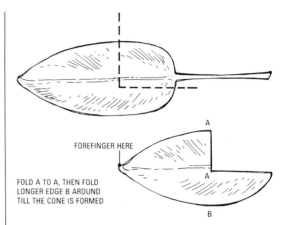

FOREFINGER HERE

FOLD A TO A, THEN FOLD
LONGER EDGE B AROUND
TILL THE CONE IS FORMED

29. *Preparation of laurel leaves for a wreath*

amaranthus. A reindeer moss base is even more appropriate to a winter tribute, as the moss is available at any time of year. The flower groups can be adapted to whatever is in season.

The informal group includes the sympathy basket, sheaf, spray, double-ended spray and posy wreath. Some people also like to include in this category flowers in cellophane and, indeed, in some areas of the country they are quite popular. It is intended that the flowers can afterwards be taken to a hospital or old peoples' home. However, there are several reasons, both ethical and artistic, why this is not appropriate. Flower bouquets in cellophane and trimmed with ribbon are generally associated with a birthday, wedding anniversary or similar celebration. Moreover, the cellophane sometimes tends to mist over which, again, is hardly appropriate to the dignity of a funeral. Also, since flowers at a funeral are intended, I believe, as a visible tribute of love and esteem to the bereaved and in memory of the deceased, they should be a gift, not a temporary loan.

FORMAL TRIBUTES

These are usually designed with a neat edging of foliage or ribbon, the base being set in one type of flower. The stems are cut fairly short so that the flower heads rest on the foam or moss. Each flower head should just touch the next one and the finished appearance should be smooth and even, so far as the flower texture will allow. When working with a foam base, be sure that the stems are long enough to bite into the foam. For a mossed base, obviously the flowers will need to be wired.

When putting the top spray on a foam base the foam should be fixed in place before the base is soaked. It can be attached with the glue gun or use the small 'bun' known as 'le Bump' supplied by the Naylorbase Organisation. This is available in three sizes with a type of screw attached which can be quickly secured to the base.

On a moss base, first soak the foam block and then take two 1.00 mm wires and tape the centre 4 cm of each wire. Bend each one in half and drive it upwards through the base of the tribute in the area where you want the top spray. Turn the tribute round the right way up so that the wires are protruding upwards and both are bedded neatly into the underside of the base (see figure 30).

Carefully impale the foam block on to the four wires till it rests on the base. Place two small pieces of stem between each pair of wires and twist once very firmly. The foam block should then be firmly fixed to the base and must not have any movement.

When designing the top spray, work mainly in the lateral, using the basic three-point technique with dimensions of one-third to two-thirds. Overall, the design should not relate to more than one-third of the total area of the tribute. This ratio should be measured by eye, for the effect will vary according to the flowers used. For example, a spray composed of red carnations will appear to be larger than one designed with alstroemeria, even though they have been made to the same dimensions.

For a cross try a monochromatic colour

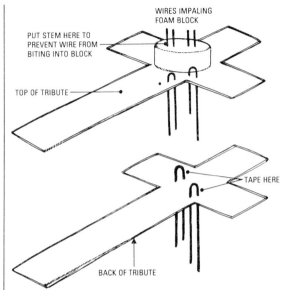

30. *Fixing a foam block on to a base for a formal tribute*

harmony of the base in cream spray chrysanthemum with a top spray of cream freesia. Add also a little solidaster and loops of bear grass.

INFORMAL TRIBUTES
Sympathy Basket

A flat-based oblong basket is the most generally used, though other more interesting shapes are sometimes appropriate, particularly when there are several ordered for the same funeral.

The basket should be prepared in the manner described on p. 55. The inner container has soaked foam taped to it and is then attached to the basket with either a glue gun or Oasis-fix. The design should be able to be seen from all angles. The basic technique used is similar to a double-ended three-point design on a lateral plane. If appropriate, a ribbon may be added. A butterfly bow in a colour toning to the flowers, should be inserted close to one side of the handle where it meets the base. The message card may also be attached at this point.

The edge flowers at either end should be on firm stems—gladioli, iris or liatris, for example. The butterfly gladiolus is particularly suitable as the stems are more slender. Roses, spray carnations and alstroemeria can be added to give strength to the centre, but there should be space between the top flower and the handle so that it can be grasped without damage.

Sheaf
This is composed of flowers usually on their natural stems which are assembled in the hand with suitable foliage. It should also be finished with an attractive ribbon bow.

Obviously strong stems are required for the longest back-flowers and delphinium, liatris, spray chrysanthemum or iris are all eminently suitable. Carnations can be used, but it is advisable lightly to wire the longest one on 0.70 mm wire just in case they snap in handling. To create a clear-cut design do not use too many types of flowers. For example, delphinium and carnations or roses, spray chrysanthemum and a few iris could be used with the addition of a little trachelium or alchemilla, September flower or slender sprays of green sedum.

Spray
The spray and the double-ended spray are designed into a foam base. These are very popular designs as they last for several days and are very natural-looking. The double-ended spray, even though an informal tribute, is frequently requested as a family tribute for the top of the casket. Ask the advice of your local funeral directors as to what height the central flowers should be for proper clearance between them and the roof of the car. It is usually about 30 cm.

This design also requires some strong-stemmed flowers to emphasise the line and size. The double-ended design looks dignified if made with one type of flower only, for instance, lilies, roses or, more simply, dahlias in varying form and size.

Posy Wreath
In appearance this is very similar to a circular centrepiece. It is usually designed on a suitable foam base; the profile is gently domed and there should be space between each flower. It is generally built up on the basis of the five-point design.

WINTER

17

FLOWERS AND FOLIAGE FOR WINTER DESIGNS

FLOWERS

During the short-day winter months, we need more than ever the uplift of a few flowers indoors; in homes, offices, waiting rooms and other public places. It is surprising what a wide variety of both flowers and foliages is still available in many flower shops, even in the depth of winter. The availability chart (see pp. 94–8) indicates what types could be accessible, though it must not be regarded as conclusive that all flowers listed are on offer from all florists all of the time, and it is inevitable that at this season of the year, the number of native flowers available is at its lowest.

Hellebores are somewhat unusual perennial plants in that they have two species flowering at this time. *Helleborus corsicus* is certainly not grown for its decorative foliage but the flowers, a clear green, are so surprising all through the winter, that it is well worth giving it garden space. Admittedly, over a few years it tends to elbow other subjects aside, for it is a vigorous grower and scatters its seeds with great profligacy. All the same, the clusters of pale green flowers are a lovely addition to any flower arrangement. They can also be wired separately for inclusion in lapel sprays and bouquets. What more could you ask of a flower growing in the open in deep winter?

The Christmas rose (*Helleborus niger*) is sometimes available to the florist from the wholesale market, particularly when ordered a few days in advance. It can be grown as a pot plant or in the garden, sometimes blooming in the most inclement weather. When the buds appear, cover them with a small cloche or glass jar to keep the flowers clean.

The florist can, of course, still rely on supplies of exotic flowers imported into this country from abroad as well as the UK growers' year-round production of staple lines like carnations and roses; and early crops of bulb flowers, too, are available in the wholesale markets.

The most ubiquitous winter flower is the spray chrysanthemum, which is one of the most adaptable of all flowers. There are the single, anemone-centred types, the spider varieties, sometimes called 'Tokyo', and the doubles. For arranging, look for stems with flowers spaced so that each flower and bud has a reasonably long stem. These are the most economical to use, for it is sometimes possible to make a modest design from just one stem. Some varieties tend to 'short break' which means that the flowers have very short stems and are bunched towards the top of the stem. This is good for very large designs, but not so helpful for a smaller arrangement. When buying spray chrysanthemums make sure that the foliage is crisp and dark green. The single varieties should have firm centres while the reverse of the double types should be just as fresh in appearance as the front of the blooms.

Lilies, also, in varying colours are available for most of the year. They are one of the most rewarding flowers for almost any type of design for, like spray chrysanthemums, they are multi-headed, with buds and open flowers as well as their own foliage.

Moreover, they offer tremendous colour power, so that just two or three added to a design contribute considerable impact.

Flower arrangers who are responsible for decorations during late autumn and early winter sometimes find it quite difficult. Frosts have probably spoilt the late dahlias and michaelmas daisy, but berried branches of, for example, *Pyracantha rogersiana* with juniper and several stems of lily 'Connecticut King' (a clear yellow) or an orange 'Prominence' or 'Enchantment' would give an impression of warmth and light. Creative use of various foliages can make the most of the limited available flower colour.

FOLIAGE

An arrangement does not necessarily have to consist of flowers plus supporting foliage to be considered a complete design, for many leaves are decorative in their own right.

The foliage available in the later part of the year is some of the most satisfactory to use for almost any design, since it is then mature and has a longer-lasting value than earlier in the year. Even so, it should still be well conditioned, using a warm solution of shrub nutrient, and carefully selected to provide variety of shape, size, colour and texture.

I was once privileged to watch a presentation by a Japanese designer who was using only foliage, working in both Western and Japanese styles. One was not even aware of the absence of flowers, for each design was totally co-ordinated and visually satisfying.

When planning any design with foliage, whether an arrangement, lapel spray or bouquet, introduce as much variety as possible, so that the design has dimension. Foliage, even though much of it is basically green, still offers an exciting range of variation in tone: some, like eucalyptus have a blue bias, others a yellow emphasis (Elaeagnus), while towards autumn and winter

many revert to bronze and red. It is sometimes even more exciting to plan an all-foliage design than one with flowers, for the colour nuances seem infinite.

Useful garden shrubs at this time include winter jasmine, the witch hazel (*Hamamelis mollis*), *Daphne mezereum*, *Prunus subhirtella* 'Autumnalis', some of the viburnums and many *Erica* cultivars. Those fortunate people who do have access to decorative garden shrubs should remember that they should be cut only sparingly in winter, but there are some that will benefit by cautious 'pruning' at this time of year: the various buddleias, for example, white, pink and deep purple; their flowers are already over, but they leave behind dark green racemes on slender stems—ideal for a shapely pedestal arrangement. For extra height, insert a few stems of late pampas. Another shrub that can be cut judiciously in late Autumn is *Leycesteria formosa*. The foliage is, by now, tough and dark green, but the interesting purple-red panicles add character to a winter design, particularly if the foliage is stripped off.

There are many evergreens which will provide material for the flower arranger in winter, including aucuba, elaeagnus, eucalyptus, holly, pittosporum, *Viburnum tinus* and the vast range of garden conifers. Also, there are still plenty of berries and fruits available to introduce a further variation of texture and colour.

A particularly decorative subject is *Stranvaesia* 'Palette' which bears colourful foliage, green, edged cream to red, all year round. It is a rather slow-growing shrub which should only be cut sparingly for the first three or four years.

Fortunately for anyone without a cutting garden, some bought foliages will last for several weeks: for example, aucuba, the spotted laurel, which is very decorative and blends well with either spray chrysanthemums or large blooms. Other winter foliages available from the flower shop are soft ruscus, eucalyptus and variegated privet plus, of course, in early December, variegated holly. The soft ruscus is particularly elegant, with many shiny green leaves on long slender stems. However, do not expect to find all these items always on offer; if you are needing foliage for a special occasion, get in touch with your supplier several weeks beforehand, to give time for some research. Generally speaking, the city florist suffers as much as the general public from a lack of interesting foliage; one problem that applies just as much to the commercial grower as to a private gardener, is that many trees and shrubs are relatively slow-growing and if cut commercially, it could be many months before they are rehabilitated. Secondly, most foliages are bulky and heavy to transport, which of course, adds to their cost.

18

SPECIAL OCCASIONS
IN WINTER

ADVENT

Like All Saints' Day, this is a big festival on the continent. In Britain, florists and flower arrangers also create designs to include four candles with seasonal flowers and foliage. Plate 27 shows a simple Advent ring based on a polystyrene wreath frame covered with scarlet ribbon. Four small blocks of dry foam were attached with a glue gun, equidistant on the base. The candles, signifying the four weeks leading up to Christmas, must be very safely fixed but while transporting designs that contain candles it is advisable to remove them. Tape three or four 1.25 mm wires about 5 cm long to each candle. These wire 'legs' drive into the foam block and through to the base. The variegated holly foliage, ribbon bows and everlasting flowers (silver poinsettia) were also attached with a glue gun.

CHRISTMAS

Advent really sets the scene for Christmas, when florists can display a wide selection of arrangements. While Advent designs are limited to the four-candle theme, Christmas displays include planted bowls of all kinds, flowering plants, particularly poinsettias, fresh flower designs, door wreaths, wall and door swags, as well as centrepieces with holly, candles and possibly some everlasting materials. This involves weeks of planning and hard work. Up to a few years ago, everything was glitter, but now the trend is for more natural effects, including foliage of all kinds, ribbons and candles.

Use them in groups as well as placed singly and they will look very attractive. Some float on water: place them with a few open short-stemmed flowers in a shallow bowl and you have an interesting centrepiece.

The Christmas door wreath is also effective if kept relatively simple. Plate 28 shows one made entirely of cupressus and decorated with a large green and scarlet ribbon, some variegated holly foliage and a few artificial berries. It is based on a single strand of heavy wire curved around into a circle and finished with a hook. The wire was then overbound with florist tape and the foliage bound directly on to it, working from the central hook down each side towards the cluster and ribbon area.

Baskets are almost always an appropriate gift, whatever the season. A presentation of flowers and fruit would be very acceptable to use as a buffet arrangement or, indeed, for someone in hospital. The design in Plate 29 is based in a large shallow basket. The flowers are set in a plastic container fixed firmly to one side of the handle while the fruit is arranged on the other side. Five scarlet roses, some yellow freesia with orange and red bouvardia are designed on an asymmetrical three-point plan. The fruit is grouped and supported with layers of paper, the out-of-season strawberries being set in a small paper frill. There can be a problem of balance when composing baskets with both fruit and flowers so it is advisable to keep checking as you add the fruit that when the design is held by the handle it does not tip.

PLATE 26

*An understated summertime wreath. On a reindeer
moss base, the three groups of flowers in
semi-parallel form include liatris, sweet William,
alstroemeria and amaranthus.*

PLATE 27

*An Advent wreath. The polystyrene ring is bound
with scarlet ribbon. Four silver candles with clusters
of variegated holly, red berries and everlasting silver
poinsettias are placed equidistant on the base.*

PLATE 28

*A simple door wreath of cupressus bound on to a
strong wire ring. The cluster of variegated holly,
and everlasting red and green berries, is emphasised
with green and scarlet ribbon.*

PLATE 29

A Christmas or New Year gift basket with red roses,
scarlet bouvardia and yellow freesia. The fruit, of
course, is optional.

PLATE 30

*Set in a plastic container on a large silver tray, this
Christmas party-time arrangement contains pink lilies
and chrysanthemums, trimmed with pink ribbons*

PLATE 31

*Bridal bouquet of mixed foliage including golden
cupressus and variegated thornless holly with a few
white roses, fruits from* Cydonia japonica, *plus
several slender branches of* Salix tortuosa *to imply
line and rhythm*

PLATE 32

*For a Christmas wedding, the bridesmaid's
pomander is a 'snowball' of white tulle with a spray
of everlasting holly and Christmas roses. Obviously,
fresh flowers can be added if preferred.*

PLATE 33

A planted bowl including calathea, hedera, begonia, saintpaulia, variegated Ficus pumila *and kalanchoe*

PARTY TIME

It is sometimes a welcome change, during the Christmas season, to have a completely simple centrepiece of fresh flowers, particularly for an engagement party or a special birthday. The design in Plate 30 is arranged on the five-point basis into a plastic container which is set on a large silver tray. The arrangement contains pink lilies and spray chrysanthemum with a few pink ribbons added in place of foliage.

WINTER WEDDINGS

With so many flowers available now for most of the year, the winter wedding can, if the customer is prepared to pay winter prices, be just as interesting and colourful as one in spring or summer. Perhaps more so, in fact, for at least we can be reasonably sure that the temperature will not be unexpectedly high. Lilies, orchids, Singapore orchids, roses and carnations are some of the many flowers suitable for brides at almost any time of the year. But possibly the winter bride wants something quite different, that is in keeping with the season.

A formal or informal bouquet of dried materials might be appropriate, particularly for a registry office wedding or one with a small number of guests. An informal bouquet can be assembled in the hand and finished with suitable ribbon (not a regular satin-finish but a narrow hessian-type.) A more formal bouquet should be based in a bouquet holder, the smallest of the Val Spicer range is most suitable. Each little group of dried materials must be cut to the required length and secured to the base with a dab from the glue gun. True, the stems must be driven into the base, but if glued as well there is no chance of their being dislodged, even in the worst of windy weather.

Many florists, as well as some brides, favour combs as the basis for a head-dress. Having consulted several hairdressers, however, I found their view to be that sometimes the combs are a problem to fix into the hair. Therefore, a head-dress based on a very light wire base is far easier to secure with several hair-grips. Wire gauge 0.46 or 0.56 will be heavy enough; tape it and then tape small groups of material to the base wire. Check as you go along, that the design is neither too soft, nor is it becoming too rigid; in the latter case, cut out the remaining wire from each little group of material so that you do not get a build-up of wire.

Should the bride want her head-dress under her veil for the ceremony, carefully but loosely stitch the design to the veil, having doubled it back to the required length. The head-dress can be hair-gripped in place and the folded-back part of the veil brought over the flowers and the face. After the ceremony the veil is folded back. The bride's veil is rather a responsibility and she may prefer to sew it herself. If the florist is entrusted with this somewhat tricky undertaking, it is important, of course, to get the measurements correct. That is, how much of the veil is wanted over the bride's face? The usual length is just below shoulder-length. If the head-dress is a circlet-type, only the front of the veil needs to be secured, for the back will be over the head-dress anyway.

Using exclusively dried flowers for a wedding certainly obviates many of the last-minute pressures so, from the florists' point of view, this would be very appropriate around Christmas-time (or near any other busy time, such as Mothers' Day or Valentine's Day.)

And as a compromise, fresh foliage and/or fresh flowers could be added at the last moment. Since wheat-ears are sometimes considered acceptable as an element in a fresh flower bouquet, then a few flowers are just as appropriate to a dried design.

A Christmas Wedding

The bouquet shown in Plate 31 was designed for a wedding taking place on the day after Christmas Day. From the florist's point of view this means that all designs must be made and delivered on Christmas Eve. The bride wore a parchment-tinted ankle-length gown with a full skirt. Several miniature roses were included in the all-foliage design with some ornamental quinces and some variegated, non-prickly holly leaves. The bouquet was made on a Val Spicer holder and lasted well for several days.

The bridesmaids wore dark green velvet and carried snowballs or pomanders, as shown in Plate 32. These were based on a small polystyrene sphere, covered first with silver paper and closely covered with tiny white tulle bows. To attach the ribbon handle tape the centre 4 cm of a 0.70 mm wire and make a multi-loop bow. First make two small loops, then a large one to form the handle and then two more to balance the first pair. Drive the wires straight through the ball until the loops are resting on top and the wire points are extending beyond the base. Return these ends neatly into the ball and the handle will be completely safe (see figure 31).

Wire the little tulle tufts with small pieces of 0.46 or 0.38 mm silver wire. The tufts are made by cutting pieces of tulle about 4 cm

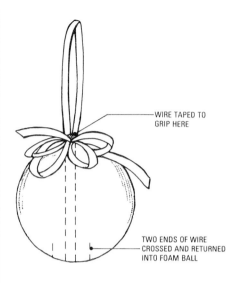

WIRE TAPED TO GRIP HERE

TWO ENDS OF WIRE CROSSED AND RETURNED INTO FOAM BALL

31. *Attaching the ribbon handle to the bridesmaid's pomander*

wide, gathering them in the centre and securing with one twist of wire, leaving about 2 cm of wire to drive into the ball. Insert them from the base and work in circles upwards to the handle. Put the tufts in very closely, so that the total effect is pure white. A spray of fresh flowers and foliage can be added at the last moment, or, as shown in the illustration, a few everlasting Christmas roses, some holly foliage and berries instead of fresh material. The ribbon loops at the base were inserted last of all.

19

DRIED FLOWERS

Dried flowers are 'in season' all the year round and most florists keep a good selection. They are particularly useful at this time of the year and it is rewarding to dry your own for this purpose. Molucella loses its clear green hue and turns a wonderful creamy-bronze while delphinium, if cut when the weather is dry, will usually retain its blue colour. If the flower is too mature, the colour fades. Achillea also keeps its golden colour and is one of the easiest subjects to dry.

Keen gardeners usually remove all dead heads as this certainly encourages more bloom as well as keeping the garden neat. But it is intersting to leave some subjects and you may find you have a number of dried flowers waiting to be harvested. Delphinium will shed its flowers but the seed heads are shapely and very useful for arrangements.

The dried calyx of a spent foxglove flower is like a little bell and these stems, also, are excellent for the main lines of a design. Aquilegia stems are very decorative once the flower has faded and left the calyx and these, also, can be left on the plant to dry naturally. Obviously in a very wet summer this would not be valid and then material should be gathered so that it can be suspended head downwards in a dry place. Crocosmia (montbretia) also dries easily and all of these will last for several years if kept clean and dry.

Queen Anne's lace which has been so lovely in the hedgerows in early summer soon dries on the stem if there is no rain. It can then be used as a line flower for large winter designs, or just one head inserted deep into an arrangement will introduce a different shape and also mask the foam to a certain extent.

Dried flower pictures look very effective when mounted in special frames that can either be constructed or bought from the wholesaler. They are actually like a shallow box so that it is possible to give the design a certain amount of depth. The back is usually plain thin wood which is not a particularly effective background for dried materials. Cover it with flock Fablon which is available in both dark green and crimson.

Assemble the main lines of the design in the hand, on the same basis as making a lapel spray. Then fix the embryo-arrangement to the base with a glue gun or other fixative. Add other pieces of material if necessary, attaching these also with glue.

Dried flowers are appropriate to many designs; they are very rewarding to work with, though it is vital to keep each type of material separate otherwise confusion may set in. Late summer is a good time to begin designing your own Christmas gifts which will be all the more appreciated if they are made with flowers from the garden. One can find other items that can be trimmed and enhanced with dried materials—for example, wall plaques and woven bases, small decorative straw rings and tiny hats which look delightful trimmed with a wreath or spray of tiny dried flowers.

It is not unknown for a bride to ask that all the bouquets be made with dried materials so that they can be kept afterwards. Certainly in extremely warm weather it is a good idea if the head-dresses for the brides-maids are made with dried flowers. And, possibly in the depth of winter, dried flower bouquets would look appropriate. Brides-maids in crimson velvet gowns could carry white or crimson muffs trimmed with a lavish spray of golden-brown dried flowers and wear head-dresses to match.

There are a number books about drying flowers and they also offer guidance on how to arrange them. This is very little different from arranging living materials except that for maximum effect one needs to work with small bunches or groups of flowers rather than with single stems.

For dried flower designs, use only dry foam, which is a different texture from the green foam intended for fresh materials. The dry foam is a little harder in texture and will not soak up water.

Masking the foam can sometimes be a problem, but one can buy very attractive reindeer moss, either the original grey, or tinted to colour-match with your design. This moss is virtually indestructible and can be used time and again. Alternatively, clean, flat green moss makes an excellent masking agent; it will dry gradually and yet still retain its green tint. Be sure to mask your base before inserting dried flowers, for if this is left until the design is almost complete, it is difficult to get between the stems without causing damage.

In the absence of any natural masking materials, ribbon could be used, but this should be very discreet. The shiny polypropylene ribbons are not really appropriate; try a hessian-look type which blends better with the character of dried flowers.

Pampas grass is wonderful for really large arrangements and can, of course, be used to introduce height to a fresh flower design. Before inserting pampas stems into the soaked foam base, wrap them with florist's tape or sellotape, so as to protect that part of the stem that will be driven into the foam. Otherwise, the stem will become soft and the pampas could keel over at an unfortunate moment.

Some very beautiful winter designs can be achieved with bare twigs, branches and, maybe, the addition of a few berried branches. As an example in nature, an oak tree in full leaf is a majestic sight, but one is unable to see the 'bone structure' of the tree. Once the leaves have fallen, the whole tracery of branches and twigs is visible. Outlined against a clear blue winter sky, or a scarlet sunset, it is a marvellous sight. In miniature, with one shapely branch plus some smaller twigs to introduce rhythm, this pattern can be imitated as the basis of a satisfying indoor design. The twisted willow, either with stripped bark or left natural, is quite wonderful for both large and smaller arrangements.

For heavy woody branches, Jumbo Oasis is excellent, as the texture is more solid than the regular type and so you will not require such a large block. Obviously, the larger the block, the more effective the masking has to be. In essence, try to use as small a block as you dare, because otherwise masking and the centre of the design tends to look somewhat stodgy.

20

GREEN AND FLOWERING PLANTS

Today, plants are an integral part of the commercial and domestic scene. But it has not always been so. The Victorians loved their plants and the homes of the upper and middle classes were rarely without their 'fernery', or at least the odd corner palm, usually a *Kentia*, or the indestructible aspidistra. The latter was the hallmark of Victorian respectability for many well-kept homes had their lace curtains discreetly drawn together with the family aspidistra enthroned on a table close to the small bay window.

The range of plants obtainable then was limited. Apart from ferns of all kinds, palms and aspidistras, creeping plants such as tradescantia were also to be seen, as well as the *Asparagus sprengeri* fern basket hanging in a sheltered doorway during the summer months.

The changes in society after World War I were reflected in public taste and, between the wars, green plants were on the decline. Fewer were sold and there was a tendency to shy away from anything Victorian. After World War II, Thomas Rochford, whose family had already been closely connected with horticulture for over 100 years, decided to develop and expand the family nurseries in the Lea Valley. Within a few years, Rochford's nurseries were responsible for producing an immense range of foliage plants, as well as the many flowering plants for which the organisation was already famous.

After years of austerity, the British public were ready for something new and the advent of these interesting foliage plants was refreshing. Foliage plants with diverse leaf shapes, sizes and colours were more than welcome. Florists were well aware of their potential and furnished their shops with this new and exciting commodity. Offices, also, began to use larger plants as space dividers to replace the impersonal plasterboard walls.

The Ford Motor Company at Dagenham commissioned a local florist to design and build an indoor garden for their new reception area. It was to be an excellent example of indoor landscaping where both management and workforce could meet on common ground in their mutual appreciation of plants. Subsequently, more examples of this type of landscaping emerged up and down the country. When the Royal Festival Hall was built trees and other large green plants were installed as an integral part of the interior decor.

Now, indoor plants still fascinate us. People living in high rise apartments or in the inner cities, still feel the need to keep in touch with living plants. It is possible to choose ones which fit the interior decor and will also adjust to your lifestyle. For example, if you are frequently away from home and have no time to care for your plants, choose a succulent such as the *Sanseveria* (mother-in-law's tongue) or a collection of cacti, for these demand minimum care and require water only now and again.

If you prefer to keep your home at a high temperature some of the more tender tropical types such as stephanotis and hibiscus would be a good choice. However, a warm home usually means a very dry

atmosphere and it may be necessary to install a humidifier to keep plants thriving.

For dedicated house plant collectors there is an excellent reference book by Dr Hessayon entitled *The House Plant Expert* which encourages, reassures and informs. There are also many others, from the popular coffee table production to the technical.

The florist should try to locate reliable growers and wholesalers from whom to buy. Production is now very specialised and so to find a good selection will mean buying through the wholesale market or visiting several growers.

All foliage and flowering plants should have a bright, fresh appearance. Foliage must be firm and clean and the plant should be completely steady in the pot. Most growers include a care card with the plant which indicates the type of environment to which it is suited. The windowsill is one of the worst places for a plant. Although there is maximum light it becomes very cold at night, while direct sunlight in the day can scorch.

Foliage plants, particularly the larger ones, are ideal for shop decor. They impart an air of elegance and can also be used to divide up areas of the shop. When plants arrive in the shop, unpack them as soon as possible. Check each one for damage and remove any paper or transparent wrapping before watering them thoroughly.

The comfortable working temperature for staff of around 10°C plus is suitable for most plants. Never store them in a cooler, nor display them outside the shop in direct sunlight or in cold and windy weather.

Check all your plants each day to see if they need watering and remove any faded flowers or foliage. Make sure that whoever is responsible for this is experienced in plant care, for even one shabby plant can ruin the whole display, not to mention the florist's reputation.

Plants deserve as much care as cut flowers in presentation and gift-wrapping. For over-the-counter sales there are plastic sleeves and containers with handles, which are very convenient for the impulse buyer.

Flowering Plants

These should be bought when they have colour visible on many of the buds and some flowers almost expanded. *Jasminum polyanthum* is one of the few plants that can be bought in bud. It is very popular as a gift for Mothering Sunday, being showy and beautifully perfumed. It will also naturalise later in the year if planted in a sheltered position. Bulb flowers, also, can be bought in bud, for once they are exposed to light, they develop all too quickly.

Azaleas should be showing colour with some buds and some developed, though not mature, flowers.

Aphelandra should have two or three flower plumes visible. The leaves must be really stiff and numerous and the plant should be neat and bushy.

Amaryllis, being a bulb flower, can be bought in tight bud, for the flowers expand fairly quickly in strong light.

Astilbe (Spiraea) The flower heads should be showing colour but not too feathery. They should be showing well above the dense foliage.

Begonia Ensure the plant is firm in its container. Buds should be showing colour with some flowers expanded.

Beloperone guttata (shrimp plant). The colourful bracts which look like shrimps are the main attraction and should be well developed.

Billbergia nutans is an unusual, but rather untidy, plant yet it has interest for the avid collector. Foliage is sharp-edged and insignificant, so buy when the crimson sheath is ready to expand and display the flowers.

Calceolaria Buy in flower.

Cineraria Flowers need to have developed but still be crisp and immature. Check foliage for whitefly; if it is present it could infect your whole stock.

Columnea Buy when almost in bloom for this is the main attraction of this plant.

Cyclamen Both flowers and foliage should be stiff and lively in appearance. There will be buds hidden amongst the leaves. The miniature types are extremely attractive and should also be bought with buds and some flowers developed.

Chrysanthemum Buy when flowers are semi-developed.

Crassula The stems should have neat spiky foliage from soil level up to the bloom.

Erica hyemalis A modestly priced bushy plant for late autumn and Christmas. The foliage should be flexible and not shedding.

Fuchsia There are so many varieties, all of which are very appealing. Buy when in bud.

Gloxinia Buy in bud. Make sure the plant is firm in the pot and that the foliage is not damaged in handling.

Genista Buy in flower. Spray foliage to increase humidity.

Hibiscus Buy in bud.

Hoya bella and H. carnosa Most flower heads should be mature. Keep away from wallpaper or from any surface that might be damaged, for this plant exudes sticky 'tears' if overwatered. Do not remove spent flower heads from *H. bella* as they fade.

Hydrangea A very popular plant in spring and summer. Buy and sell in bloom. Never let the soil dry out and keep the plant away from draught where the flower heads will shrivel. Stand the plant upside-down in a bucket of clear water and this should revive it.

Impatiens (Busy Lizzie) Buy in bud.

Jasminum polyanthum Buy in bud.

Kalanchoe blossfeldiana A useful, modestly priced plant mainly seen in winter, particularly at Christmas. Buy in bloom and check that the foliage is plentiful and dark green.

Poinsettia The traditional Christmas plant. The red, white or pink bracts should be fully developed and the foliage dark green and plentiful.

Primula Buy in bloom but before the flowers are completely mature.

Pelargonium Buy when just coming into flower.

Saintpaulia (African violet) Make sure that the flower heads are not submerged by too many leaves. Buy with both buds and flowers visible and remove spent flowers so that others can develop.

Stephanotis Buy with both buds and flowers showing.

Solanum (Winter cherry) Another cheap and very cheerful plant at Christmas-time. Berries should be bright orange and plentiful. Foliage must be dense and shiny dark green. Berries are thought to be poisonous.

Zygocactus (Christmas cactus) Buy when buds show colour with some flowers also. Once set in place, this plant does not like to be moved, for this could inhibit or retard flowering.

Planted Bowls

Planted bowls usually have a minimum of three plants, according to the size of container. The objective is to create a composition with colour and texture variation, but also there must be compatibility between the plants. They should all have similar requirements for water, light and warmth. Also the growing rates must be considered and a very fast-growing subject should not be included with those that develop more slowly, otherwise they could become smothered. Before planting, put the chosen subjects into the container in various positions to judge what the best arrangement would be.

For variation in height select several plants that thrive close to the rim of the container, such as saintpaulia, ivy, variegated *Ficus pumila* and kalanchoe (see Plate 33). A small-flowering geranium gives colour at mid-height while the central foliage plant, a calathea, provides maximum height, as well as some colour with the deep red reverse of the foliage.

First put small crocks or charcoal into the container. Then add a thin layer of compost. Position the central tallest plant first, then the pelargonium, working down in layers towards the outer rim of the container. The saintpaulia, the ficus and the ivy were tilted slightly outwards to provide maximum colour impact. Add compost as each plant is inserted, pressing it down firmly but making sure it is not too tightly packed. Finish the top with moss if required. This should be at least 1 cm below the rim of the bowl otherwise water may run over the edge. If possible, leave any planted arrangement for one or two days before selling or delivery so that the plants have time to settle. Add a ribbon bow if it seems appropriate.

Dish Garden

This is self-explanatory for it is a design based in a shallow dish, as opposed to a bowl, with suitable foliage and flowering plants which are usually fairly small. Cactus, echeverias and similar plants are suitable as well as miniature evergreens. Possibly a 'lake' of mirror glass can be inserted, with paths, a bridge and so on, though the accessories should never outweigh the plant interest.

Terrariums

These are available in varying shapes and sizes but all have a very small aperture, the idea being that the plants will generate their own humidity and therefore the planting will require minimum maintenance. Ample time and patience is required for planting though there are special long-handled mini-tools that will secure the plant and release it when placed in the terrarium. Choose the selection with great care, for if one should grow too rapidly, it will take charge and completely submerge the others.

A few suggestions include *Ficus pumila*, cryptanthus, fittonia, and several of the peperomia family, preferably *P. metallica*, *variegata* or *caperata*. These will supply a little

height to the planting but do not grow too vigorously.

Hanging Containers

There are many types including those made from basket and macramé and they furnish the flower shop most effectively. In the home one can progress one's plant collection beyond the windowsill and table top to hooks and hangers in all kinds of places. Unfortunately this sometimes presents a problem for watering but there are even some containers now that can be winched up and down from the ceiling. Some mail order catalogues offer poles that can be extended to fit exactly between floor and ceiling. Three or four hooks are attached at intervals to the pole on which more plants can be suspended. This is extremely effective, particularly when positioned near an unfurnished corner.

For hanging containers, the choice of subjects is very wide including *Cissus rhombifolia*, the grape ivy, and *Cissus antarctica*, the kangaroo vine, both of which are tolerant of situations away from direct light but need plenty of water. *Chlorophytum*, spider plant, *Philodendron oxycardium* and scindapsus are also very undemanding, providing that they are watered about twice a week.

Ferns will tolerate a shady situation away from direct window light; *Nephrolepis*, *Asparagus plumosus* and *A. sprengeri* being three of the most easy-going. Ivies and tradescantia are fast-growing but prefer direct light.

Out of Doors

Hanging baskets, window boxes and tubs are ideal for people with no gardens or a very small patch. For winter furnishing plant small evergreen shrubs such as *Buxus* (box) or variegated *Euonymus*. Pyramid bay is elegant but very expensive—they are sometimes chained to railings in cities as they tend to vanish overnight!

In about mid-November, tubs and

windowboxes can be planted with early-flowering bulbs such as daffodils, narcissus and hyacinth. Towards the end of May plant geraniums in variety which will provide a veritable riot of colour throughout the summer. Nepeta is a good-natured trailing plant which, together with marigolds and the dark blue lobelia grows generously. Trailing nasturtiums are also attractive, but for colour value and minimum care, geraniums prove the most rewarding.

While geraniums tolerate very sunny conditions, *Impatiens* (busy Lizzie) prefer not to be in bright sunlight. They need to be watered regularly and will produce rich colour in situations where few other plants would thrive. *Impatiens* can be grown from seed but for an 'instant garden' it is better to buy small plants with an established root system.

Fuchsias, both standard and trailing, are very popular for baskets and tubs. They are beautiful flowers but hate wind and need regular watering every day.

AVAILABILITY CHART
(APPROXIMATE ONLY)

	Jan	Feb	Mar	Apr	May	June	July	Aug	Sept	Oct	Nov	Dec
ACHILLEA					★	★	★	★	★			
ACONITE	★	★										
AGAPANTHUS					★	★	★	★	★			
ALCHEMILLA					★	★	★					
ALLIUM					★	★	★	★				
ALSTROEMERIA	★	★	★	★	★	★	★	★	★	★	★	★
AMARANTHUS						★	★	★	★	★		
ANEMONE	★	★	★	★	★				★	★	★	★
ANIGOZANTHOS (Kangaroo Paw)	★	★	★	★	★							
ANTHURIUM	★	★	★	★	★	★	★	★	★	★	★	★
ANTIRRHINUM					★	★	★	★	★			
ARUM LILY	★	★	★	★	★	★					★	★
ARUM, wild		★	★									
ASPARAGUS PLUMOSUS	★	★	★	★	★	★	★	★	★	★	★	★
ASPARAGUS SPRENGERI	★	★	★	★	★	★	★	★	★	★	★	★
ASPLENIUM (garden fern)					★	★	★	★	★			
ASTER ERICOIDUS (September flower)					★	★	★	★	★	★		
ASTILBE (spiraea)					★	★	★	★	★			

	Jan	Feb	Mar	Apr	May	June	July	Aug	Sept	Oct	Nov	Dec
AZALEA	★	★									★	★
BEECH foliage							★	★	★			
BEGONIA rex, etc.	★	★	★	★	★	★	★	★	★	★	★	★
BLUEBELL				★	★							
BOUVARDIA			★	★	★	★	★	★	★	★	★	★
CAMPANULA					★	★						
CARNATION	★	★	★	★	★	★	★	★	★	★	★	★
CHINCHERINCHEE	★	★	★	★	★	★	★	★	★	★	★	★
CHLOROPHYTUM	★	★	★	★	★	★	★	★	★	★	★	★
CHRYSANTHEMUM, bloom								★	★	★	★	★
CHRYSANTHEMUM, spray	★	★	★	★	★	★	★	★	★	★	★	★
CORNFLOWER				★	★	★	★					
COWSLIP				★	★							
CROCOSMIA (Montbretia)							★	★	★			
CUCKOO FLOWER					★	★						
CYCLAMEN	★	★	★	★				★	★	★	★	★
CYMBIDIUM orchid	★	★	★							★	★	★
DAFFODIL	★	★	★	★								★
DAHLIA								★	★	★		
DELPHINIUM					★	★	★					
DENDROBIUM (Singapore orchid)	★	★	★	★	★	★	★	★	★	★	★	★
ECHEVERIA	★	★	★	★	★	★	★	★	★	★	★	★
EREMURUS						★	★					

	Jan	Feb	Mar	Apr	May	June	July	Aug	Sept	Oct	Nov	Dec
EUCALYPTUS	★	★	★	★	★	★	★	★	★	★	★	★
EUPHORBIA FULGENS	★							★	★	★	★	★
FICUS, various	★	★	★	★	★	★	★	★	★	★	★	★
FORSYTHIA	★	★	★	★	★							
FOXGLOVE (digitalis)					★	★	★					
FREESIA	★	★	★	★	★	★	★	★	★	★	★	★
GARDENIA	★	★	★	★	★							
GERANIUM					★	★	★	★	★			
GERBERA	★	★	★	★	★	★	★	★	★	★	★	★
GLADIOLUS						★	★	★	★	★	★	
GRAPE HYACINTH (Muscari)				★	★							
GYPSOPHILA	★	★	★	★	★	★	★	★	★	★	★	★
HELLEBORUS FOETIDUS		★	★	★	★	★						
HELLEBORUS NIGER	★											★
HELECONIA	★	★	★	★	★	★	★	★	★	★	★	★
HOLLY	★	★	★	★	★	★	★	★	★	★	★	★
HONEYSUCKLE, wild							★	★				
HOSTA						★	★	★	★			
HYACINTH	★	★	★	★								★
INCENSE POPLAR				★	★	★	★					
IRIS	★	★	★	★	★	★	★	★	★	★	★	★
IVY (hedera), various	★	★	★	★	★	★	★	★	★	★	★	★
IXIA			★	★	★	★	★					

	Jan	Feb	Mar	Apr	May	June	July	Aug	Sept	Oct	Nov	Dec
JASMINE, yellow.winter	★	★									★	★
JASMINE, white (*J. officinale*)			★	★	★	★	★					
KALANCHOE	★	★	★	★	★	★				★	★	★
LOOSESTRIFE					★	★						
LIATRIS	★	★	★	★	★	★	★	★	★	★	★	★
LILAC	★	★	★	★	★							
LILY, various	★	★	★	★	★	★	★	★	★	★	★	★
LILY-OF-THE-VALLEY (Convallaria) commercial	★	★	★	★	★	★	★	★	★	★	★	★
LOVE-IN-A-MIST (Nigella)						★	★	★				
MIMOSA	★											★
MOLUCELLA	★	★	★	★	★	★	★	★	★	★	★	★
MONTE CASSINO (September flower)	★	★	★	★	★		★	★	★	★	★	
NARCISSUS	★	★	★	★								★
NERINE			★	★	★	★	★	★				
ORCHIDS, Singapore	★	★	★	★	★	★	★	★	★	★	★	★
PAEONY				★	★							
PARSLEY, wild (Queen Anne's lace)					★	★						
PHILADELPHUS					★	★						
PITTOSPORUM	★	★	★	★						★	★	★
POINSETTIA	★	★	★	★							★	★
POLYANTHUS	★	★	★	★	★							★
PROTEA	★	★						★	★	★	★	★

	Jan	Feb	Mar	Apr	May	June	July	Aug	Sept	Oct	Nov	Dec
PRUNUS	★	★	★									
RANUNCULUS				★	★							
ROSES	★	★	★	★	★	★	★	★	★	★	★	★
SAINTPAULIA (African violet)	★	★	★	★	★	★	★	★	★	★	★	★
SALIX TORTUOSA					★	★	★	★	★	★		
SEPTEMBER FLOWER (Aster ericoide)					★	★	★	★	★	★		
SOLIDASTER			★	★	★	★	★	★	★	★	★	
SNOWDROP (Galanthus)	★	★	★									
STATICE								★	★	★		
STEPHANOTIS			★	★	★	★			★	★		
STOCK (Matthiola incarna)			★	★	★	★	★					
STRELITZIA	★	★	★	★	★	★	★	★	★	★	★	★
SWEET PEA (Lathyrus)				★	★	★	★					
SWEET WILLIAM						★	★					
TRACHELIUM					★	★	★	★	★	★	★	★
TULIP	★	★	★	★	★							★
WALLFLOWER				★	★							
VIBURNUM OPULUS (snowball tree)				★	★							
VIBURNUM TINUS	★	★	★	★	★	★	★	★	★	★	★	★
WEIGELA				★	★	★	★	★				
ZINNIA							★	★	★			

GLOSSARY

ADJACENT
In colour harmony, refers to those tints near to, and on one side only, of a primary or secondary colour.

ADVENT
The beginning of the Christian church's year, including the four Sundays preceding Christmas.

ALL-SAINTS DAY
The first Sunday in November; recognised in Europe as a special day for taking flowers and tributes to family graves.

ANALOGOUS
Colour harmony consisting of those tints adjoining each other on one or on either side of a primary colour, but not to extend so as to include a second primary colour, i.e., yellow to orange.

ASYMMETRICAL
A design each side of which is different in line and emphasis and possibly in content, but which combines to make a pleasing visual whole.

AUTO-CORSO
A car bonnet decoration, usually for weddings. The base, of Oasis foam encased in plastic mesh, has a large rubber sucker on the underside enabling it to be attached to any smooth surface.

AYR
Florists' abbreviation of all-year-round (spray chrysanthemum).

BACKBONE
The strong main line at the back or in the centre of an arrangement.

BACKING
The neat finish on the reverse of a funeral tribute, e.g. wreath or cushion.

BIEDERMEIER
A circular classic design made either in the hand or in a formal container. Material is placed closely together, though not usually in concentric circles. The name derives from Count Biedermeier, a renowned furniture designer of the 19th century.

BLOOMFIX
Flower foam (English manufacture) both for fresh and dried materials.

BOUQUET HOLDER
Plastic and foam container into which a bouquet can be constructed.

BOX PLEATING
An elegant form of ribbon trimming that provides an attractive edge to funeral tributes.

BULLDOG CLIP
Large clip used to hold papers together.

BUTTERFLY BOW
A simple two or four-loop bow either tied in the centre or fixed with a taped wire.

BUTTONHOLE (BOUTONNIÈRE)
Usually a single flower, perhaps with a little foliage, suitable to be worn on the lapel of a jacket.

CAKE TOP
An arrangement of fresh flowers designed for the top of a bridal cake.

CALYX
The green 'cup' surrounding the petals in a bud, and the base of the petals in an open flower.

CARE CARD
Card accompanying a gift of cut flowers or a plant with instructions on how to take care of it.

CARPETING
Inserting flower heads on very short stems close to one another to form a solid base.

CHAPLET
A memorial design usually based with laurel or other long-lasting foliage. A flower spray is sometimes added at the base and military or ceremonial ribbons added.

CHRYSAL
A brand of flower nutrient.

CLEAR-LIFE
A brand-name clear spray that can be applied to mature flowers to prevent petals shedding. It is intended to 'hold' the flower for a day or so at a particular level of maturity to suit the design. It is not a pick-me-up for fading flowers.

COLOUR HARMONY
The relationship of one or more colours to others. This is an elusive quality since few people see colour in the same way.

COLOUR WHEEL
The formal arrangement of basic colours, both primary and secondary, as seen in a rainbow.

COMPLEMENTARY COLOUR HARMONY
The use of two colours opposite each other on the colour wheel, e.g. violet and yellow.

CROSS
The traditional formal funeral tribute. Flowers or foliage based closely to follow the form of the cross, or can be inserted in open form, but should still maintain the shape and proportion of the base.

CUSHION
A formal tribute, edged with either ribbon or foliage or both and with a top spray of flowers which should be one-third or less the total area of the base. The base is closely set with flowers to resemble fabric (carpeting).

DECIDUOUS
A tree, shrub or plant that sheds its leaves during winter.

DECORATIVE DESIGN
Flowers and foliage placed in the design to achieve a particular effect. The material can be seasonal and out-of-season and possibly not inserted in accordance with its natural growing habit, i.e., gladioli placed horizontally.

DE-FOLIATE
To remove all leaves.

DE-THORN
To remove all thorns, in particular, from a rose stem.

DISH GARDEN
Decorative arrangement of small plants and suitable accessories in a shallow container. The plants should still be on their roots.

DOMINANT FLOWERS
The most important flowers in an arrangement; dominant by virtue of size, colour or texture, or all three.

DRY FOAM
Foam into which everlasting materials can be arranged.

EDGING
Pleated ribbon or long-lasting foliage, or both, for trimming the edge of a formal tribute such as a wreath or cushion.

EDWARDIAN POSY
A round bouquet held in the hand, the flowers and foliage placed closely, but not in circles, nor so tightly-packed as in the Victorian posy.

EQUIPMENT
All the various items required in the day-to-day running of a flower shop.

FACING DESIGN
An arrangement with the main interest towards the front.

FIBRE
A special mixture for growing bulbs, usually when planted in small containers for indoors.

FLORAL FOAM
A synthetic material into which flowers and foliage can be arranged.

FLORIBUNDA
A cultivated hybrid rose whose flowers grow in clusters or sprays.

FLORIST'S TAPE
Narrow tape used to seal the stem-end after the flower or floret has been wired, and for covering the wire.

FOAM BASE
Usually refers to a funeral tribute base such as wreath, cushion or heart.

FOCAL POINT
Central point of visual interest of a design.

FREEZER TAPE
Strongly adhesive tape for use in freezers.

FROG
Small plastic base with four prongs on to which the foam is impaled.

GATES OF HEAVEN
An elaborate type of funeral tribute still popular in some areas, but very rarely requested.

GIFT WRAP
Usually cellophane embellished with ribbon trimmings.

GLUE GUN
An electric gun which heats glue sticks so that the liquid can be controlled to a fine jet by means of the trigger. Very useful for work with everlasting materials.

GUTTA PERCHA
A type of florist's tape.

HAIRPINS
Wires cut short and bent double.

HAND-TIED BOUQUET
Flowers and foliage assembled in the hand, the stems being placed parallel from the perpendicular so that they eventually form a spiral around the holding point. The finished design is tied securely in this place and the stems all cut to one length. The bouquet is then ready to be stood in a container without further arranging or manipulation.

HANGING CONTAINERS
Wire or plastic containers large enough to contain several decorative plants, for use either outside or indoors.

HEART, FUNERAL
A solid or outline design, usually based with one type of flower in the carpeting technique and with a small top spray of special flowers added.

HOOK METHOD
Wire inserted into the flower stem and up through the centre of the flower. A small hook is made with the top of the wire which is gently retracted so that the hook rests within the centre of the flower. This method is only possible if the flower stem is hollow which means that the wiring is totally invisible.

INTERNAL WIRING
A wire inserted inside the flower stem up into the flower head (see hook method) thus making the wire invisible.

JUMBO OASIS
A special type of foam in very large blocks used for particularly big display designs.

LAPEL SPRAY
A small assembly of flowers, foliage and buds to be worn on the lapel.

LATERAL
Material placed at an angle to the main central line, i.e., towards the side.

LAUREL PINNING
Individual laurel leaves pinned to a base, usually a wreath or chaplet.

LINE FLOWERS
Materials used to define the line of the design.

MARKET COUNTS
The mandatory quantity of stems of one type of flower sold in a wholesale market.

MASKING
Covering the foam base of any design so that it is not visible through the design.

MASKING TAPE
Wide tape used to protect a surface, for instance, glass or special wood.

MESSAGE CARD
The card attached to a gift or funeral tribute.

MONOCHROMATIC COLOUR HARMONY
Tints, tones and shades of one colour.

MOTHERING SUNDAY
In most countries a fixed date, not tied to the church calendar as in Britain.

MOTHERS' DAY
In Britain, the fourth Sunday in Lent and, therefore, not a fixed date.

N.A.F.A.S.
National Association of Flower Arrangement Societies.

NAYLOR BASES
The brand-name for particular types of funeral bases, available in various shapes and sizes.

NODE
The point on a stem from which a leaf grows.

NUTRIENT SOLUTION
See Chrysal.

OASIS-FIX
An oil-based adhesive on a reel, used for attaching one dry surface to another, e.g. an Oasis-prong to the inside of a container.

OASIS-TAPE
Tape, either green or white, for fixing foam firmly into a container.

PEAK TIMES
Special seasons, e.g., Christmas, Valentine's Day, when more people than usual buy flowers and plants.

POTENTIAL VASE LIFE
The estimated number of days a flower will last, i.e., give pleasure to the client or recipient.

ROSE HIPS
Decorative fruits that develop on some varieties of rose after the blooms have faded.

SEPAL
Part of the calyx.

SUPPLIERS

Tribute Bases

Millfield Florist Sundries Limited, Peterborough, Cambridgeshire.

James Naylor, Limited, Redditch, Worcestershire.

Foam

Bloomfix/Florafoam, Baxenden Chemicals Limited, Accrington, Lancashire.

Smithers Oasis UK Limited

Bouquet Holders

Smithers Oasis UK Limited

Val Spicer Designs, Tavistock, Devon.

Foliage

Strongs Greenery, Clonegal, Bunclody, Co. Wexford, Ireland.

The above sources supply on a wholesale basis only.

Floristry Magazines

The Florist Trade Magazine, 120 Lower Ham Road, Kingston-on-Thames, Surrey.

The Flower Trades Journal, 17 Wickham Road, Beckenham, Kent.

The Professional Floral Designer, P.O. Box 12309, Oklahoma City, OK.73157-2309 U.S.A.

BIBLIOGRAPHY

Der Florist Ingeborg Wundermann

Dictionary of Floristry and Flower Arrangement Anthony Gatrell

Field Guide to the Wild Flowers of Britain (Readers Digest)

Flowers of the World Frances Perry V.M.H.

The Hillier Colour Dictionary of Trees and Shrubs

The House Plant Expert Dr D. G. Hessayon

Gerard's *Herball*

INDEX